JN418758

TOP
LEVEL
WRITING
SENSE
THE TWO
For Elite Group
II

TOP LEVEL **WRITING** SENSE
THE TWO
For Elite Group

초판 1쇄 발행 2007년 8월 31일

지은이 한일
펴낸이 신성현 • 오상욱
만든이 홍수인 • 박진아
펴낸곳 도서출판 아이엠북스
121-884 서울시 마포구 연남동 567-39 302호
Tel. 02)3141-9508 Fax. 02)3141-9504
북디자인 A&A 에이앤에이 디자인
Tel. 02)2285-2022 Fax. 02)2285-2023
출판등록 2006년 6월 7일 제 313-2006-000122호
ISBN 978-89-92334-30-3 14740

www.iambooks.co.kr

Written by **IL HAN**

Iam books

Contents

Composition & Character

The purpose of this practice is to have you experience the high level of writing and ready for the studying in a higher educational institution.

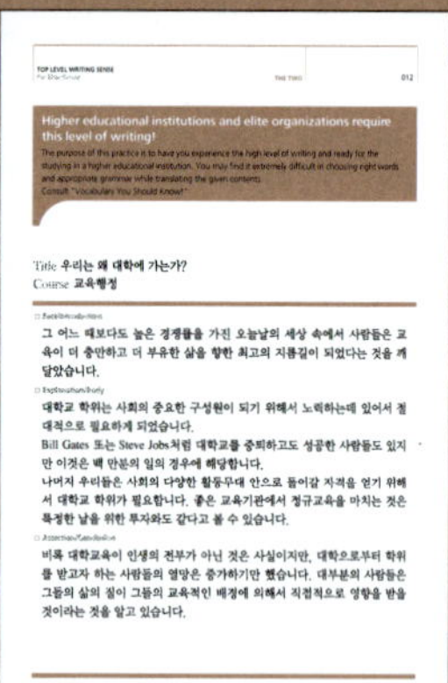

TOP LEVEL WRITING SENSE | THE TWO | 012

Higher educational institutions and elite organizations require this level of writing!

The purpose of this practice is to have you experience the high level of writing and ready for the studying in a higher educational institution. You may find it extremely difficult in choosing right words and appropriate grammar while translating the given contents.
Consult "Vocabulary You Should Know!"

Title **우리는 왜 대학에 가는가?**
Course **교육행정**

그 어느 때보다도 높은 경쟁률을 가진 오늘날의 세상 속에서 사람들은 교육이 더 충만하고 더 부유한 삶을 향한 최고의 지름길이 되었다는 것을 깨달았습니다.

대학교 학위는 사회의 중요한 구성원이 되기 위해서 노력하는데 있어서 절대적으로 필요하게 되었습니다.
Bill Gates 또는 Steve Jobs처럼 대학교를 중퇴하고도 성공한 사람들도 있지만 이것은 백 만분의 일의 경우에 해당합니다.
나머지 우리들은 사회의 다양한 활동무대 안으로 들어갈 자격을 얻기 위해서 대학교 학위가 필요합니다. 좋은 교육기관에서 정규교육을 마치는 것은 특정한 날을 위한 투자와도 같다고 볼 수 있습니다.

비록 대학교육이 인생의 전부가 아닌 것은 사실이지만, 대학으로부터 학위를 받고자 하는 사람들의 열망은 증가하기만 했습니다. 대부분의 사람들은 그들의 삶의 질이 그들의 교육적인 배경에 의해서 직접적으로 영향을 받을 것이라는 것을 알고 있습니다.

The listed vocabulary follows the sequence of the content, not randomly mixed. This will help you find the appropriate vocabulary for your writing. Vocabulary here is not only helpful for the given writing but also leading you to the place where you are to be intelligent and educated.

Title **Why do we go to College?**
Course **Educational Administration** | Target 01 | 013

Vocabulary You Should Know!

The listed vocabulary follows the sequence of the content, not randomly mixed. This will help you find the appropriate vocabulary for your writing. Vocabulary here is not only helpful for the given writing but also leading you to the place where you are to be intelligent and educated. Remember that they are the suggestions. You can have your own choices of vocabulary for the writing which might be more acceptable than the suggested one.

- ever-increasing
- competition
- latest
- shortcut
- rewarding
- diploma
- absolutely
- essential
- quest
- valued member
- dropouts
- one-in-a-million
- rest
- gain
- admission
- arenas
- formal education
- recognized institution
- investment
- du jour
- desire
- obtain
- Majority
- quality of life
- educational

This is one of the translations for the given material. It is worth noting that many expressions used here are the professional level. Since you are assumed to write it in your own level, you should not blame yourself when you see differences between your writing and this article.

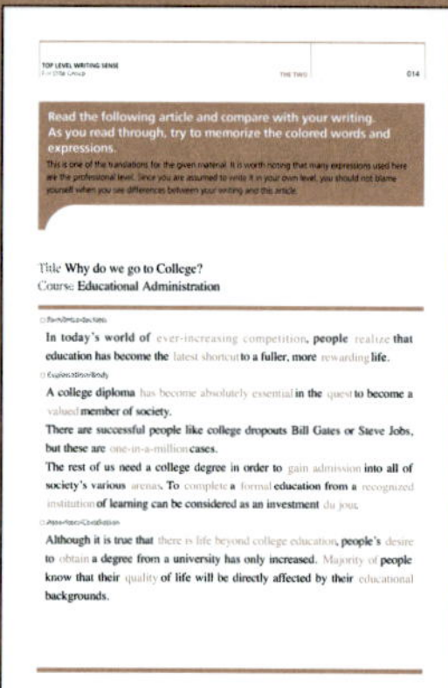

TOP LEVEL WRITING SENSE | THE TWO | 014

Read the following article and compare with your writing. As you read through, try to memorize the colored words and expressions.

This is one of the translations for the given material. It is worth noting that many expressions used here are the professional level. Since you are assumed to write it in your own level, you should not blame yourself when you see differences between your writing and this article.

Title **Why do we go to College?**
Course **Educational Administration**

In today's world of ever-increasing competition, people realize that education has become the latest shortcut to a fuller, more rewarding life.

A college diploma has become absolutely essential in the quest to become a valued member of society.
There are successful people like college dropouts Bill Gates or Steve Jobs, but these are one-in-a-million cases.
The rest of us need a college degree in order to gain admission into all of society's various arenas. To complete a formal education from a recognized institution of learning can be considered as an investment du jour.

Although it is true that there is life beyond college education, people's desire to obtain a degree from a university has only increased. Majority of people know that their quality of life will be directly affected by their educational backgrounds.

Try to find easier vocabulary and expressions for the blank than you have written previously. You can see what is academic and what is casual. This practice enhances your memory of the words and its practicality. You can also have a clear understanding for the synonyms.

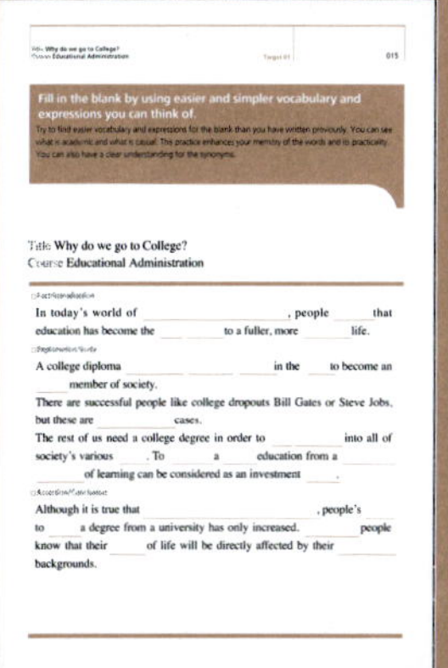
015

Fill in the blank by using easier and simpler vocabulary and expressions you can think of.

Try to find easier vocabulary and expressions for the blank than you have written previously. You can see what is academic and what is casual. This practice enhances your memory of the words and its practicality. You can also have a clear understanding for the synonyms.

Title Why do we go to College?
Course Educational Administration

In today's world of ____, people ____ that education has become the ____ ____ to a fuller, more ____ life.

A college diploma ____ ____ ____ in the ____ to become an ____ member of society.
There are successful people like college dropouts Bill Gates or Steve Jobs, but these are ____ cases.
The rest of us need a college degree in order to ____ ____ into all of society's various ____. To ____ a ____ education from a ____ ____ of learning can be considered as an investment ____.

Although it is true that ____, people's ____ to ____ a degree from a university has only increased. ____ people know that their ____ of life will be directly affected by their ____ backgrounds.

Compare the vocabulary and phrases here with those you have used previously.

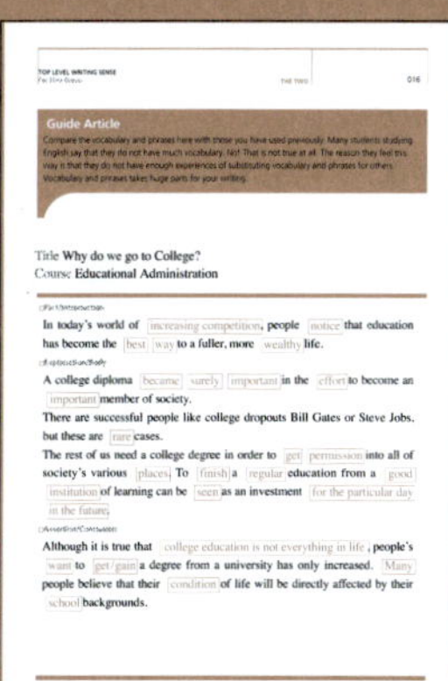
TOP LEVEL WRITING SENSE

016

Guide Article

Compare the vocabulary and phrases here with those you have used previously. Many students studying English say that they do not have much vocabulary. No! That is not true at all. The reason they feel this way is that they do not have enough experiences of substituting vocabulary and phrases for others. Vocabulary and phrases takes huge parts for your writing.

Title Why do we go to College?
Course Educational Administration

In today's world of increasing competition, people notice that education has become the best way to a fuller, more wealthy life.

A college diploma became surely important in the effort to become an important member of society.
There are successful people like college dropouts Bill Gates or Steve Jobs, but these are rare cases.
The rest of us need a college degree in order to get permission into all of society's various places. To finish a regular education from a good institution of learning can be seen as an investment for the particular day in the future.

Although it is true that college education is not everything in life, people's want to get/gain a degree from a university has only increased. Many people believe that their condition of life will be directly affected by their school backgrounds.

What can be used as a substitute of the word and phrase below? Feel free to refer to the previous article.

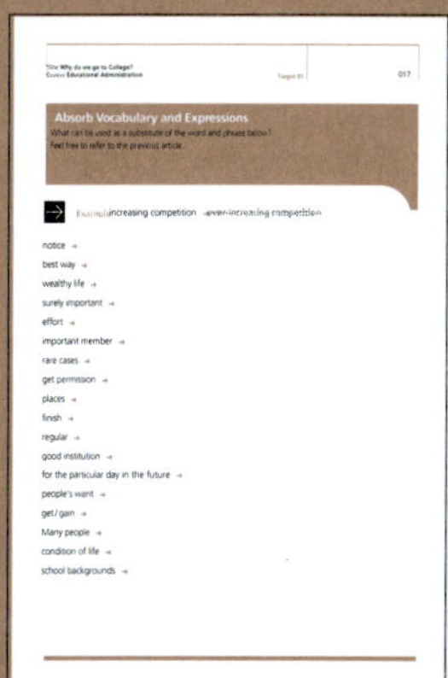
Title Why do we go to College?
Course Educational Administration

017

Absorb Vocabulary and Expressions

What can be used as a substitute of the word and phrase below?
Feel free to refer to the previous article.

Example increasing competition → ever-increasing competition

notice →
best way →
wealthy life →
surely important →
effort →
important member →
rare cases →
get permission →
places →
finish →
regular →
good institution →
for the particular day in the future →
people's want →
get / gain →
Many people →
condition of life →
school backgrounds →

Composition & Character

Make a sentence that contains the given word and phrase. Use the given words for any parts of speech such as a subject, verb, object, preposition object etc.

Change the colored words and expressions to more difficult and academic ones! Knowing only one word for the writing will limit your skill, so you should have the alternatives. This practice will lead you to the state-of-art academic and formal writing.

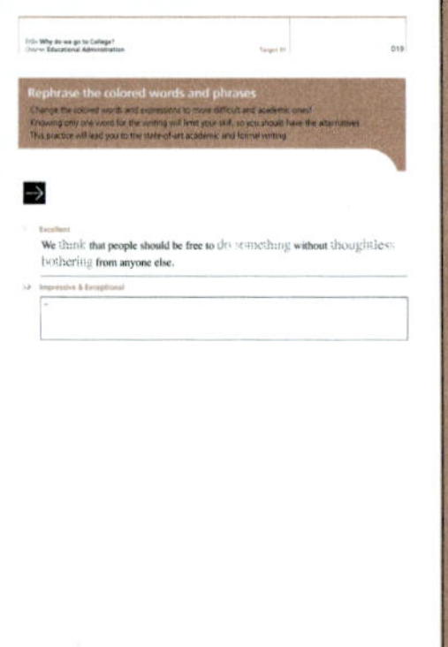

You can find more reading materials in this website and expand your knowledge for the rapidly changing world.

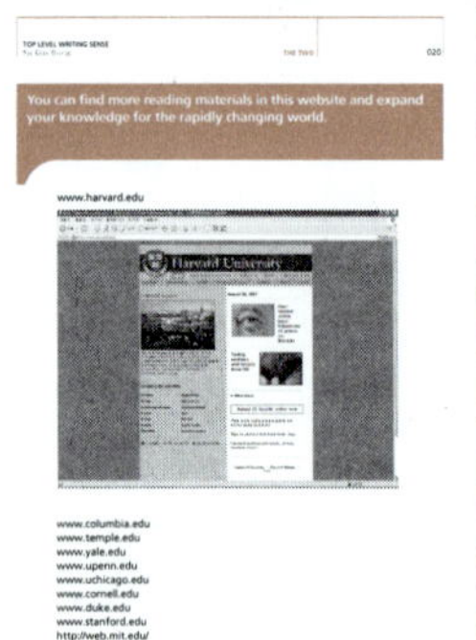

Guideline

Level

Senior in University
TOEFL 6.0
4 years of studying in English speaking countries

Approximate word counts

131 words

Required Skill

Ready to use commonly used Academic idioms and expressions such as "ever-increasing," "college dropout," "one-in-a million," "du jour," "kaleidoscope," etc.

Target 01

Higher educational institutions and elite organizations require this level of writing!

The purpose of this practice is to have you experience the high level of writing and ready for the studying in a higher educational institution. You may find it extremely difficult in choosing right words and appropriate grammar while translating the given contents.
Consult "Vocabulary You Should Know!"

Title 우리는 왜 대학에 가는가?
Course 교육행정

□ Fact/Introduction

그 어느 때보다도 높은 경쟁률을 가진 오늘날의 세상 속에서 사람들은 교육이 더 충만하고 더 부유한 삶을 향한 최고의 지름길이 되었다는 것을 깨달았습니다.

□ Explanation/Body

대학교 학위는 사회의 중요한 구성원이 되기 위해서 노력하는데 있어서 절대적으로 필요하게 되었습니다.

Bill Gates 또는 Steve Jobs처럼 대학교를 중퇴하고도 성공한 사람들도 있지만 이것은 백 만분의 일의 경우에 해당합니다.

나머지 우리들은 사회의 다양한 활동무대 안으로 들어갈 자격을 얻기 위해서 대학교 학위가 필요합니다. 좋은 교육기관에서 정규교육을 마치는 것은 특정한 날을 위한 투자와도 같다고 볼 수 있습니다.

□ Assertion/Conclusion

비록 대학교육이 인생의 전부가 아닌 것은 사실이지만, 대학으로부터 학위를 받고자 하는 사람들의 열망은 증가하기만 했습니다. 대부분의 사람들은 그들의 삶의 질이 그들의 교육적인 배경에 의해서 직접적으로 영향을 받을 것이라는 것을 알고 있습니다.

Vocabulary You Should Know!

The listed vocabulary follows the sequence of the content, not randomly mixed. This will help you find the appropriate vocabulary for your writing. Vocabulary here is not only helpful for the given writing but also leading you to the place where you are to be intelligent and educated. Remember that they are the suggestions. You can have your own choices of vocabulary for the writing which might be more acceptable than the suggested one.

- ▷ ever-increasing
- ▷ competition
- ▷ latest
- ▷ shortcut
- ▷ rewarding
- ▷ diploma
- ▷ absolutely
- ▷ essential
- ▷ quest
- ▷ valued member
- ▷ dropouts
- ▷ one-in-a-million
- ▷ rest
- ▷ gain
- ▷ admission
- ▷ arenas
- ▷ formal education
- ▷ recognized institution
- ▷ investment
- ▷ du jour
- ▷ desire
- ▷ obtain
- ▷ Majority
- ▷ quality of life
- ▷ educational

**Read the following article and compare with your writing.
As you read through, try to memorize the colored words and expressions.**

This is one of the translations for the given material. It is worth noting that many expressions used here are the professional level. Since you are assumed to write it in your own level, you should not blame yourself when you see differences between your writing and this article.

Title Why do we go to College?
Course Educational Administration

□ Fact/Introduction

In today's world of ever-increasing competition, people realize that education has become the latest shortcut to a fuller, more rewarding life.

□ Explanation/Body

A college diploma has become absolutely essential in the quest to become a valued member of society.

There are successful people like college dropouts Bill Gates or Steve Jobs, but these are one-in-a-million cases.

The rest of us need a college degree in order to gain admission into all of society's various arenas. To complete a formal education from a recognized institution of learning can be considered as an investment du jour.

□ Assertion/Conclusion

Although it is true that there is life beyond college education, people's desire to obtain a degree from a university has only increased. Majority of people know that their quality of life will be directly affected by their educational backgrounds.

Fill in the blank by using easier and simpler vocabulary and expressions you can think of.

Try to find easier vocabulary and expressions for the blank than you have written previously. You can see what is academic and what is casual. This practice enhances your memory of the words and its practicality. You can also have a clear understanding for the synonyms.

Title Why do we go to College?
Course Educational Administration

□ Fact/Introduction

In today's world of ______________________, people ______ that education has become the ___ ______ to a fuller, more _______ life.

□ Explanation/Body

A college diploma ________ _______ _____ in the ____ to become an _____ member of society.

There are successful people like college dropouts Bill Gates or Steve Jobs, but these are ____________ cases.

The rest of us need a college degree in order to ___ _______ into all of society's various ____ . To ______ a _____ education from a ________ _______ of learning can be considered as an investment ____ .

□ Assertion/Conclusion

Although it is true that _________________________, people's _____ to _____ a degree from a university has only increased. ________ people know that their _____ of life will be directly affected by their ________ backgrounds.

Guide Article

Compare the vocabulary and phrases here with those you have used previously. Many students studying English say that they do not have much vocabulary. No! That is not true at all. The reason they feel this way is that they do not have enough experiences of substituting vocabulary and phrases for others. Vocabulary and phrases takes huge parts for your writing.

Title Why do we go to College?
Course Educational Administration

□ Fact/Introduction

In today's world of [increasing competition], people [notice] that education has become the [best] [way] to a fuller, more [wealthy] life.

□ Explanation/Body

A college diploma [became] [surely] [important] in the [effort] to become an [important] member of society.

There are successful people like college dropouts Bill Gates or Steve Jobs, but these are [rare] cases.

The rest of us need a college degree in order to [get] [permission] into all of society's various [places]. To [finish] a [regular] education from a [good] [institution] of learning can be [seen] as an investment [for the particular day in the future].

□ Assertion/Conclusion

Although it is true that [college education is not everything in life], people's [want] to [get/gain] a degree from a university has only increased. [Many] people believe that their [condition] of life will be directly affected by their [school] backgrounds.

Absorb Vocabulary and Expressions

What can be used as a substitute of the word and phrase below?
Feel free to refer to the previous article.

Example increasing competition → **ever-increasing competition**

notice →

best way →

wealthy life →

surely important →

effort →

important member →

rare cases →

get permission →

places →

finish →

regular →

good institution →

for the particular day in the future →

people's want →

get / gain →

Many people →

condition of life →

school backgrounds →

Create Your Own Sentence

-Make a sentence that contains the given word and phrase.
-Use the given words for any parts of speech such as a subject, verb, object, preposition object etc.
-You can change the form of the words.

1 ever-increasing competition

▶

2 essential

▶

3 valued member

▶

4 One-in-a-million cases

▶

5 college degree

▶

6. society's various arenas

▶

7 formal education

▶

8 Although

▶

9 people's desire

▶

10 majority

▶

Rephrase the colored words and phrases

Change the colored words and expressions to more difficult and academic ones!
Knowing only one word for the writing will limit your skill, so you should have the alternatives.
This practice will lead you to the state-of-art academic and formal writing.

> **Excellent**

We think that people should be free to do something without thoughtless bothering from anyone else.

>> **Impressive & Exceptional**

▶

You can find more reading materials in this website and expand your knowledge for the rapidly changing world.

www.harvard.edu

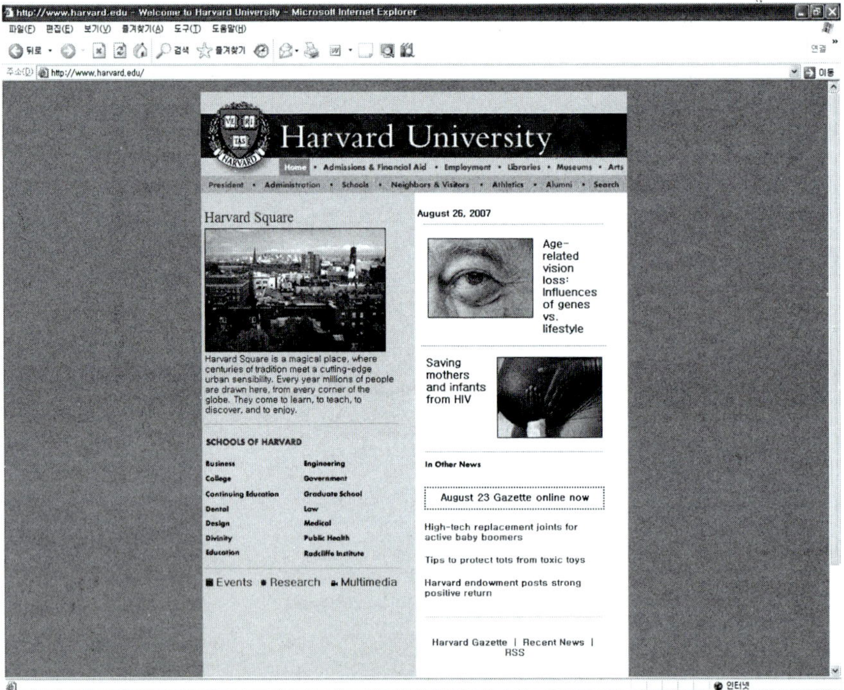

www.columbia.edu
www.temple.edu
www.yale.edu
www.upenn.edu
www.uchicago.edu
www.cornell.edu
www.duke.edu
www.stanford.edu
http://web.mit.edu/
www.brown.edu
www.universityofcalifornia.edu
www.smc.edu

Level

Junior in University
TOEFL 6.0
2 years of studying in English speaking countries

Approximate word counts

134 words

Required Skill

Required to use some sociological terminologies such as, "Animal activists," "protectionists," "slaughtering," "uncivilized," "chief aim," "ill treatment," "sustained efforts," "status symbols," "extinct," "indiscreet exploitation."

Target 02

Higher educational institutions and elite organizations require this level of writing!

The purpose of this practice is to have you experience the high level of writing and ready for the studying in a higher educational institution. You may find it extremely difficult in choosing right words and appropriate grammar while translating the given contents.
Consult "Vocabulary You Should Know!"

Title 제품생산과 동물학대
Course 동물학

□ Fact/Introduction

동물 보호주의자라고 간혹 불리는 동물 보호운동가들은 사치용품을 위해서 동물을 학대하는 것을 반대합니다. 이러한 활동가들은 개인생활용품을 생산하기 위해서 동물들을 도살(盜殺)하는 것은 야만적인 행동이라고 비난합니다.

□ Explanation/Body

이러한 비평가들은 동물들에 대한 학대를 방지할 목적으로 런던에 동물학대방지 협회(S.P.C.A)를 조직했습니다. 이 조직의 주된 목적은 연구기관의 동물학대를 신고하고 지역사회를 교육하는 것입니다. 그러나, 부단한 노력에도 불구하고, 동물로부터 만들어진 제품의 생산은 급등하고 있습니다, 왜냐하면 사람들이 물건을 일상용품으로뿐만 아니라 신분표시로도 구입하기 때문입니다.

□ Assertion/Conclusion

결과적으로, 해마다 수백 가지의 가정용품이 식물들과 동물들로부터 만들어지고 있으며 거의 3분의 1에 해당하는 지구의 멸종동물들이 무분별한 제품생산과 관계가 있습니다.

Vocabulary You Should Know!

The listed vocabulary follows the sequence of the content, not randomly mixed. This will help you find the appropriate vocabulary for your writing. Vocabulary here is not only helpful for the given writing but also leading you to the place where you are to be intelligent and educated. Remember that they are the suggestions. You can have your own choices of vocabulary for the writing which might be more acceptable than the suggested one.

- ▷ animal activists
- ▷ referred
- ▷ protectionists
- ▷ oppose
- ▷ abuse
- ▷ luxury
- ▷ articles
- ▷ criticize
- ▷ slaughtering
- ▷ manufacture
- ▷ personal care goods
- ▷ uncivilized
- ▷ behavior
- ▷ critics
- ▷ organized
- ▷ S.P.C.A(the Society for the Prevention of Cruelty to Animals)
- ▷ object
- ▷ preventing
- ▷ cruelty
- ▷ chief
- ▷ aim
- ▷ organization
- ▷ accusing
- ▷ ill treatment
- ▷ institution
- ▷ educating
- ▷ local community
- ▷ sustained
- ▷ animal-derived
- ▷ sharply
- ▷ purchase
- ▷ daily use
- ▷ status
- ▷ symbols
- ▷ household
- ▷ nearly
- ▷ one third
- ▷ extinct animals
- ▷ in connection with
- ▷ indiscreet

Read the following article and compare with your writing. As you read through, try to memorize the colored words and expressions.

This is one of the translations for the given material. It is worth noting that many expressions used here are the professional level. Since you are assumed to write it in your own level, you should not blame yourself when you see differences between your writing and this article.

Title Manufacturing goods and animal abuse
Course Zoology

□ Fact/Introduction

Animal activists, sometimes referred as animal protectionists, oppose the animal abuse for the use of luxury articles. These activists criticize that the slaughtering of animals to manufacture personal care goods is an uncivilized behavior.

□ Explanation/Body

These critics have organized S.P.C.A(*the Society for the Prevention of Cruelty to Animals*) in London with the object of preventing cruelty toward animals. The chief aim of this organization is accusing ill treatment of animals in the research institution, and educating the local community. However, despite its sustained efforts, manufacturing animal-derived products is rising sharply because people purchase goods not only for daily use but also for the status symbols.

□ Assertion/Conclusion

Consequently each year hundreds of household products are made from plants and animals, and nearly one third of extinct animals on earth are in connection with the indiscreet manufactures of products.

Fill in the blank by using easier and simpler vocabulary and expressions you can think of.

Try to find easier vocabulary and expressions for the blank than you have written previously. You can see what is academic and what is casual. This practice enhances your memory of the words and its practicality. You can also have a clear understanding for the synonyms.

Title Manufacturing goods and animal abuse
Course Zoology

□ Fact/Introduction

Animal activists, sometimes ______ as animal protectionists, ______ the animal abuse for the use of ______ ______. These activists ______ that the ______ of animals to ______ personal care goods is a ______ ______.

□ Explanation/Body

These critics have ______ S.P.C.A(*the Society for the Prevention of Cruelty to Animals*) in London with the ______ of ______ cruelty ______ animals. The ____ ____ of this ______ is ______ ____ ______ of animals in the ______, and ______ the local community. ______, despite its ______ ______, ______ animal-derived ______ is ______ ______ because people ______ goods not only for ____ use but also for the ______ ______.

□ Assertion/Conclusion

Consequently each year ______ household ______ are made from plants and animals, and ______ one third of ______ animals on earth ______ the ______ ______ of ______.

Guide Article

Compare the vocabulary and phrases here with those you have used previously. Many students studying English say that they do not have much vocabulary. No! That is not true at all. The reason they feel this way is that they do not have enough experiences of substituting vocabulary and phrases for others. Vocabulary and phrases takes huge parts for your writing.

Title Manufacturing goods and animal abuse
Course Zoology

□ **Fact/Introduction**

Animal activists, sometimes called as animal protectionists, are against the animal abuse for the use of expensive items. These activists blame that the killing of animals to make personal care goods is a barbaric act.

□ **Explanation/Body**

These critics have set up S.P.C.A(*the Society for the Prevention of Cruelty to Animals*) in London with the purpose of stopping cruelty to animal. The main purpose of this group is reporting bad care of animals in the laboratory and teaching the local community. But, despite its constant tries, making animal-derived items is increasing rapidly because people buy goods not only for everyday use but also for the class mark.

□ **Assertion/Conclusion**

Consequently each year many household goods are made from plants and animals, and almost one third of vanished animals on earth are related with the thoughtless producing of items.

Absorb Vocabulary and Expressions

What can be used as a substitute of the word and phrase below?
Feel free to refer to the previous article.

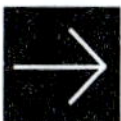

Example called → **referred**

expensive items →

blame →

killing →

make →

barbaric act →

set up S.P.C.A →

purpose →

stopping cruelty →

main purpose →

group →

reporting bad care →

teaching →

constant tries →

making →

animal-derived items →

increasing →

rapidly →

buy →

everyday use →

class mark →

many household goods →

almost →

vanished →

are related with →

thoughtless →

producing →

Create Your Own Sentence

-Make a sentence that contains the given word and phrase.
-Use the given words for any parts of speech such as a subject, verb, object, preposition object etc.
-You can change the form of the words.

1 animal abuse

▸

2 criticize

▸

3 personal care goods

▸

4 uncivilized behavior

▸

5 chief aim

▸

6. sustained efforts

▸

7 animal-derived products

▸

8 status symbols

▸

9 extinct animals

▸

10 indiscreet

▸

Rephrase the colored words and phrases

Change the colored words and expressions to more difficult and academic ones!
Knowing only one word for the writing will limit your skill, so you should have the alternatives.
This practice will lead you to the state-of-art academic and formal writing.

> Excellent

Almost half of the world's people live in the fifty underdeveloped countries, nations

>> Impressive & Exceptional

▶

> Excellent

with poor industries in which serious lack of need is the everyday life.

>> Impressive & Exceptional

▶

You can find more reading materials in this website and expand your knowledge for the rapidly changing world.

http://www.choosecrueltyfree.org.au/animals.html

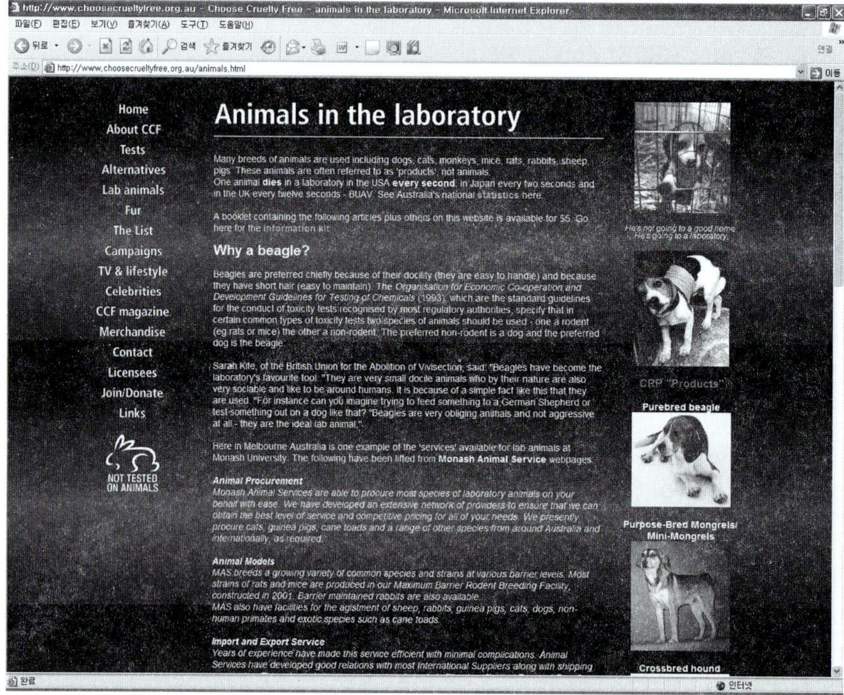

Animals in the laboratory

Many breeds of animals are used including dogs, cats, monkeys, mice, rats, rabbits, sheep, pigs. These animals are often referred to as 'products', not animals.
One animal **dies** in a laboratory in the USA **every second**, in Japan every two seconds and in the UK every twelve seconds - BUAV. See Australia's national statistics here.

A booklet containing the following articles plus others on this website is available for $5. Go here for the information kit.

Why a beagle?

Beagles are preferred chiefly because of their docility (they are easy to handle) and because they have short hair (easy to maintain). *The Organisation for Economic Co-operation and Development Guidelines for Testing of Chemicals* (1993), which are the standard guidelines for the conduct of toxicity tests recognised by most regulatory authorities, specify that in certain common types of toxicity tests two species of animals should be used - one a rodent (eg rats or mice) the other a non-rodent. The preferred non-rodent is a dog and the preferred dog is the beagle.

Sarah Kite, of the British Union for the Abolition of Vivisection, said: "Beagles have become the laboratory's favourite tool. "They are very small docile animals who by their nature are also very sociable and like to be around humans. It is because of a simple fact like this that they are used. "For instance can you imagine trying to feed something to a German Shepherd or test something out on a dog like that? "Beagles are very obliging animals and not aggressive at all - they are the ideal lab animal,".

Here in Melbourne Australia is one example of the 'services' available for lab animals at Monash University. The following have been lifted from **Monash Animal Service** webpages.

Animal Procurement
Monash Animal Services are able to procure most species of laboratory animals on your behalf with ease. We have developed an extensive network of providers to ensure that we can obtain the best level of service and competitive pricing for all of your needs. We presently procure cats, guinea pigs, cane toads and a range of other species from around Australia and internationally, as required.

Animal Models
MAS breeds a growing variety of common species and strains at various barrier levels. Most strains of rats and mice are produced in our Maximum Barrier Rodent Breeding Facility, constructed in 2001. Barrier maintained rabbits are also available.
MAS also have facilities for the agistment of sheep, rabbits, guinea pigs, cats, dogs, non-human primates and exotic species such as cane toads.

Import and Export Service
Years of experience have made this service efficient with minimal complications. Animal Services have developed good relations with most International Suppliers along with shipping

Level

Freshmen ~ Sophomore in University
TOEFL 6.0
1 year of studying in English speaking countries

Approximate word counts

134 words

Required Skill

Key words "Either," "guided by," "melted," "significance," "Gradually," "a key cause," "rapid breakdown," "flocked," "supervision of," "mass production."

Target 03

Higher educational institutions and elite organizations require this level of writing!

The purpose of this practice is to have you experience the high level of writing and ready for the studying in a higher educational institution. You may find it extremely difficult in choosing right words and appropriate grammar while translating the given contents.
Consult "Vocabulary You Should Know!"

Title 전통의 붕괴
Course 산업화

□ Fact/Introduction

지역사회가 크든 작든 그 사회 속 깊이 녹아 있는 전통들에 의해서 인도를 받습니다. 아쉽게도 이러한 전통들은 그것의 의미를 잃어버리기 시작했습니다.

□ Explanation/Body

수 초안에 사진이나 문서를 보낼 수 있는 전화기, 팩스, 그리고 복사기 같은 새로운 발명품들의 소개는 사람들의 만남을 단절시켰고 이것은 전통의 빠른 붕괴를 촉진(促進)하는 주요 원인이 되었습니다.
이러한 변화들과 함께, 사람들은 새로운 직장과 생활양식을 찾기 위해서 도시로 몰려들게 되었고, 도시는 풍부한 노동력을 가지게 되었습니다.

□ Assertion/Conclusion

사람들이 회사 소유자들에게 자신들의 노동력을 팔기를 원할 때 그들은 낯선 사람들의 감독을 받기를 꺼리지 않았습니다. 결국, 이러한 모든 변화들이 합쳐져서 대량생산이라는 새로운 생산 시스템을 만들게 되었고 지역사회는 전통보다는 생산성에 더 관심을 갖는 단체가 되었습니다.

Vocabulary You Should Know!

The listed vocabulary follows the sequence of the content, not randomly mixed. This will help you find the appropriate vocabulary for your writing. Vocabulary here is not only helpful for the given writing but also leading you to the place where you are to be intelligent and educated. Remember that they are the suggestions. You can have your own choices of vocabulary for the writing which might be more acceptable than the suggested one.

- ▷ either
- ▷ communities
- ▷ guided
- ▷ melted
- ▷ losing
- ▷ significance
- ▷ gradually
- ▷ inventions
- ▷ facsimile
- ▷ transmit
- ▷ documents
- ▷ disconnected
- ▷ contact
- ▷ key
- ▷ cause
- ▷ prompts
- ▷ rapid
- ▷ breakdown
- ▷ flocked
- ▷ search
- ▷ abundant
- ▷ labor
- ▷ willing
- ▷ under
- ▷ supervision
- ▷ mass
- ▷ production
- ▷ interested
- ▷ productivity

Read the following article and compare with your writing. As you read through, try to memorize the colored words and expressions.

This is one of the translations for the given material. It is worth noting that many expressions used here are the professional level. Since you are assumed to write it in your own level, you should not blame yourself when you see differences between your writing and this article.

Title Breakdown of Tradition
Course Industrialization

□ Fact/Introduction

Either big or small, communities are guided by the traditions, melted deep in the society. Sadly these traditions began losing their significance.

□ Explanation/Body

The introduction of new inventions such as the telephone, the facsimile, and the copy machine that can transmit pictures and documents within seconds has disconnected personal contact and it has become a key cause that prompts a rapid breakdown of traditions.

Along with these changes, people flocked to the cities to search for new jobs and lifestyles, and cities had abundant labor force.

□ Assertion/Conclusion

As people wanted to sell their labor force to the company owners, they were willing to be under the supervision of strangers. In a result, all these changes together made the new system of production-mass production, and communities have become a group that is more interested in productivity than tradition.

Fill in the blank by using easier and simpler vocabulary and expressions you can think of.

Try to find easier vocabulary and expressions for the blank than you have written previously. You can see what is academic and what is casual. This practice enhances your memory of the words and its practicality. You can also have a clear understanding for the synonyms.

Title Breakdown of Tradition
Course Industrialization

□ Fact/Introduction

________, ________ are ______ by the traditions, ______ deep in the society. Sadly these traditions began ______ their ________.

□ Explanation/Body

The ________ of new ________ such as the telephone, the facsimile, and the copy machine that can ______ pictures and ________ ______ seconds has ________ personal ______ and it has become ______ ______ that ______ a ______ ________ of traditions.

________ these changes, people ______ to the cities to ______ for new jobs and ______, and cities had ______ labor ______.

□ Assertion/Conclusion

As people wanted to sell their labor ______ to the company owners, they ______ ______ to be under the ________ of strangers. In a result, all these changes together made the new ______ of production-mass production, and ________ have become a group that is more interested in ________ than tradition.

Guide Article

Compare the vocabulary and phrases here with those you have used previously. Many students studying English say that they do not have much vocabulary. No! That is not true at all. The reason they feel this way is that they do not have enough experiences of substituting vocabulary and phrases for others. Vocabulary and phrases takes huge parts for your writing.

Title Breakdown of Tradition
Course Industrialization

□ **Fact/Introduction**

Whether it is big or small, societies are led by the traditions, embedded deep in the society. Sadly these traditions began to lose their importance.

□ **Explanation/Body**

The emergence of new devices such as the telephone, the facsimile, and the copy machine that can send pictures and written papers in seconds has blocked personal touch and it has become a main reason that stimulate a fast destruction of traditions.

With these changes, people rushed to the cities to look for new jobs and living patterns and cities had plentiful labor force.

□ **Assertion/Conclusion**

As people wanted to sell their labor power to the company owners, they wanted to be under the order of strangers. In a result, all these changes together made the new structure/method of production-mass production, and society have become a group that is more interested in efficiency than tradition.

Absorb Vocabulary and Expressions

What can be used as a substitute of the word and phrase below?
Feel free to refer to the previous article.

Example Either big or small → **Whether it is big or small**

societies →

led by →

embedded →

importance →

emergence →

devices →

send →

written papers →

blocked →

personal touch →

main →

reason →

stimulate →

fast destruction →

with these changes →

rushed →

look →

living patterns →

plentiful →

power →

wanted to →

order →

new structure / method →

efficiency →

Create Your Own Sentence

-Make a sentence that contains the given word and phrase.
-Use the given words for any parts of speech such as a subject, verb, object, preposition object etc.
-You can change the form of the words.

1 Either

▶

2 transmit

▶

3 within

▶

4 a key cause

▶

5 prompts

▶

6. rapid

▶

7 breakdown

▶

8 abundant

▶

9 mass production

▶

10 productivity

▶

Rephrase the colored words and phrases

Change the colored words and expressions to more difficult and academic ones!
Knowing only one word for the writing will limit your skill, so you should have the alternatives.
This practice will lead you to the state-of-art academic and formal writing.

> Excellent

When factory developed across England and the Europe countries,

>> Impressive & Exceptional

▶

> Excellent

cities got bigger to the size that had never existed before.

>> Impressive & Exceptional

▶

You can find more reading materials in this website and expand your knowledge for the rapidly changing world.

http://www.siliconvalley.com/

Level

Freshmen in University
TOEFL 6.0
10 months~1 year of studying in English speaking countries

Approximate word counts

134 words

Required Skill

Be aware of some commonly used words / expressions such as "categorizes," "in any shape or so," "blue collar worker," "extend." High-intermediate level of grammar

Target 04

Higher educational institutions and elite organizations require this level of writing!

The purpose of this practice is to have you experience the high level of writing and ready for the studying in a higher educational institution. You may find it extremely difficult in choosing right words and appropriate grammar while translating the given contents.
Consult "Vocabulary You Should Know!"

Title 사회계층에 따른 대우
Course 사회학

□ Fact/Introduction

사회계층은 피할 수 없습니다. 우리가 어디에 있든 또는 우리가 누구든 우리는 우리의 신분을 분류하는 특정한 장소 안에 있게 됩니다.

□ Explanation/Body

우리가 어떤 형태로든 수입이 있는 한 우리는 상류층, 중류층, 또는 하류층이라는 세 가지 계층가운데 있습니다. 우리가 더 나은 교육을 추구할지 말지 그것은 우리의 결정입니다, 그러나 우리는 고등학교 졸업자, 대학교졸업자, 아니면 박사학위수여자처럼 우리의 교육수준에 의해서 판단되는 것으로부터 자유롭지 않습니다. 직업도 예외가 아닙니다. '블루 칼라 노동자'라는 용어 그리고 '화이트 칼라 노동자'라는 용어는 우리 직업의 일반적인 설명이 되었습니다.

□ Assertion/Conclusion

우리의 수입, 교육, 또는 직업에 의지해서 사회계층을 평가하는 것이 문제가 되는 것은 아닙니다. 문제는 우리가 사람들의 권리와 가치를 그들의 계층에 따라 다르게 평가할 때 발생합니다.

Vocabulary You Should Know!

The listed vocabulary follows the sequence of the content, not randomly mixed. This will help you find the appropriate vocabulary for your writing. Vocabulary here is not only helpful for the given writing but also leading you to the place where you are to be intelligent and educated. Remember that they are the suggestions. You can have your own choices of vocabulary for the writing which might be more acceptable than the suggested one.

- ▷ social classes
- ▷ inevitable
- ▷ No matter ~
- ▷ categorizes
- ▷ status
- ▷ as long as
- ▷ shape or form
- ▷ upper class
- ▷ middle class
- ▷ lower class
- ▷ pursue
- ▷ higher education
- ▷ being judged by
- ▷ doctorates
- ▷ occupation
- ▷ exceptional
- ▷ collar
- ▷ descriptions
- ▷ of our job
- ▷ extend
- ▷ assess
- ▷ depending on
- ▷ arises
- ▷ evaluate
- ▷ value
- ▷ differently
- ▷ according to

**Read the following article and compare with your writing.
As you read through, try to memorize the colored words and expressions.**

This is one of the translations for the given material. It is worth noting that many expressions used here are the professional level. Since you are assumed to write it in your own level, you should not blame yourself when you see differences between your writing and this article.

Title Treatment according to Social Class
Course Sociology

□ Fact/Introduction

Social classes are inevitable. No matter where we are, or who we are, we are in a certain place that categorizes our status.

□ Explanation/Body

As long as we have some income in any shape or form, we are among the three classes - upper class, middle class, or lower class. It should be our decision whether we pursue the higher education or not, but we are not free from being judged by our education level such as high school graduates, college graduates, or doctorates. Occupation is not exceptional. The terms 'blue collar worker' and 'white collar worker' has become the general descriptions of our job.

□ Assertion/Conclusion

It does not extend to be a problem to assess the social class depending on our income, education, or occupation. A problem arises when we evaluate people's right and value differently according to their classes.

Fill in the blank by using easier and simpler vocabulary and expressions you can think of.

Try to find easier vocabulary and expressions for the blank than you have written previously. You can see what is academic and what is casual. This practice enhances your memory of the words and its practicality. You can also have a clear understanding for the synonyms.

Title Treatment according to Social Class
Course Sociology

□ Fact/Introduction

Social classes are ________ . No matter where we are, or who we are, we are in a certain place that ________ our status.

□ Explanation/Body

As long as we have some ______ in any _____ or ____ , we are among the three classes - _____ class, middle class, or _____ class. It should be our ______ whether we ______ the higher education or not, but we are not free from being ______ by our education level such as high school graduates, college graduates, or doctorates. ________ are not ________ . The ______ 'blue collar worker' and 'white collar worker' has become the ______ ________ of our job.

□ Assertion/Conclusion

It does not ________ a problem to _____ the social class ________ our ______ , education, or ________ . A problem _____ when we ______ people's right and _____ differently ________ their classes.

Guide Article

Compare the vocabulary and phrases here with those you have used previously. Many students studying English say that they do not have much vocabulary. No! That is not true at all. The reason they feel this way is that they do not have enough experiences of substituting vocabulary and phrases for others. Vocabulary and phrases takes huge parts for your writing.

Title Treatment according to Social Class
Course Sociology

□ Fact/Introduction

Social classes are unavoidable . No matter where we are, or who we are, we are in a certain place that divides our status.

□ Explanation/Body

As long as we have some earnings in any type or way , we are among the three classes - higher class, middle class, or working class. It should be our plan whether we seek the higher education or not, but we are not free from being considered by our education level such as high school graduates, college graduates, or doctorates. Jobs are not the special case . The words 'blue collar worker' and 'white collar worker' has become the common explanation of our job.

□ Assertion/Conclusion

It does not become a problem to evaluate the social class according to our earnings , education, or jobs . A problem begins when we estimate people's right and importance differently along with their classes.

Absorb Vocabulary and Expressions

What can be used as a substitute of the word and phrase below?
Feel free to refer to the previous article.

Example unavoidable → **inevitable**

divides →

earnings →

any type or way →

higher class →

working class →

plan →

seek →

considered by →

Jobs →

the special case →

words →

common →

explanation of our job →

become a problem →

evaluate →

according to →

begins →

estimate →

importance →

Create Your Own Sentence

-Make a sentence that contains the given word and phrase.
-Use the given words for any parts of speech such as a subject, verb, object, preposition object etc.
-You can change the form of the words.

1 social status

▸

2 upper class

▸

3 our decision

▸

4 whether

▸

5 higher education

▸

6. occupation

▸

7 general descriptions

▸

8 extend

▸

9 assess

▸

10 people's right

▸

Rephrase the colored words and phrases

Change the colored words and expressions to more difficult and academic ones! Knowing only one word for the writing will limit your skill, so you should have the alternatives.
This practice will lead you to the state-of-art academic and formal writing.

> Excellent

Although people sometimes joke that "money won't buy joy,"

>> Impressive & Exceptional

▸

> Excellent

most anxiously want fortune all the same.

>> Impressive & Exceptional

▸

You can find more reading materials in this website and expand your knowledge for the rapidly changing world.

www.beverlyhills.org

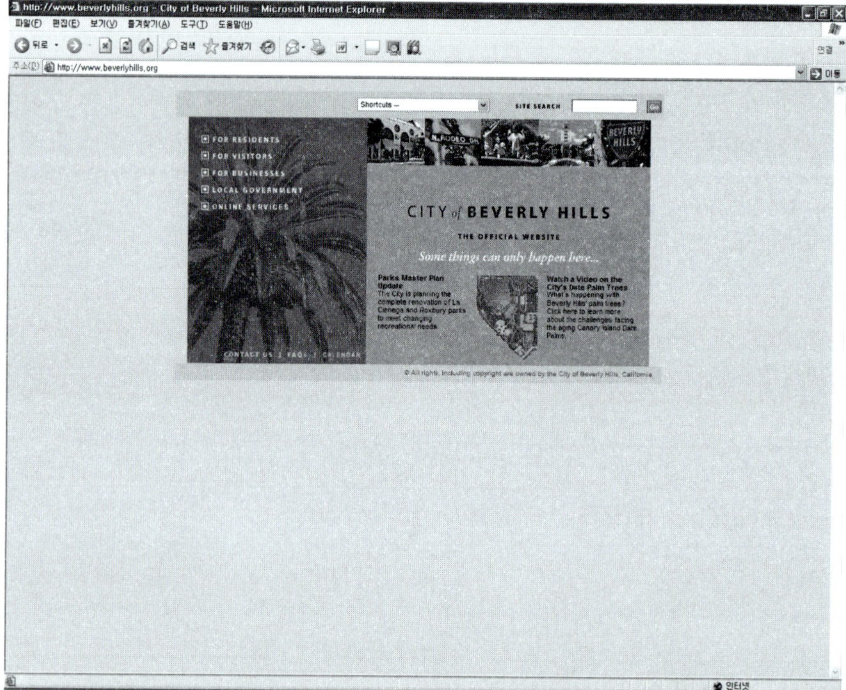

Level

Freshmen in University
TOEFL 6.0
10 month and 1 year of studying in English speaking countries

Approximate word counts

136 words

Required Skill

Moderate level in word choices.
Demonstrating the fundamental level of grammar use.

Target 05

Higher educational institutions and elite organizations require this level of writing!

The purpose of this practice is to have you experience the high level of writing and ready for the studying in a higher educational institution. You may find it extremely difficult in choosing right words and appropriate grammar while translating the given contents.
Consult "Vocabulary You Should Know!"

Title 환경변화, 물 부족
Course 환경과학

□ Fact/Introduction

인간은 지금 수십 년 전에는 상상도 할 수 없었던 문제들에 직면하고 있습니다. 그 가운데 하나가 물 부족입니다. 우리는 물 공급의 부족을 경험하고 있습니다.

□ Explanation/Body

비의 부족이 이러한 지구상의 물 부족의 중심에 있습니다. 지구온난화(地球溫暖化) 현상 때문에 지구의 기후가 바뀌었습니다. 건기(乾期)가 더 길어지고 우기(雨期)가 더 짧아졌습니다. 그들의 생존을 빗물에 의지하고 있는 동물들과 가축들은 이러한 불규칙하고 예측하기 어려운 날씨형태로 인해 그들의 생활환경에 심한 변화를 겪고 있습니다.

□ Assertion/Conclusion

결과적으로, 이러한 메마른 땅에 사는 가축의 몸 크기는 다른 지역에 있는 가축의 몸 크기보다 더 작습니다. 이러한 가축으로부터의 우유는 양적(量的)으로나 질적(質的)으로 기준에 못 미칩니다. 결국 소의 우유를 거의 매일 마시는 인간들은 이러한 변화의 영향을 지대(至大)하게 받고 있습니다.

Vocabulary You Should Know!

The listed vocabulary follows the sequence of the content, not randomly mixed. This will help you find the appropriate vocabulary for your writing. Vocabulary here is not only helpful for the given writing but also leading you to the place where you are to be intelligent and educated. Remember that they are the suggestions. You can have your own choices of vocabulary for the writing which might be more acceptable than the suggested one.

- ▷ facing
- ▷ unimaginable
- ▷ shortage
- ▷ deficiency
- ▷ supply
- ▷ center
- ▷ climate
- ▷ global warming
- ▷ dry season
- ▷ rainy season
- ▷ relying
- ▷ rainwater
- ▷ existence
- ▷ severe
- ▷ environment
- ▷ due to
- ▷ irregular
- ▷ unpredictable
- ▷ Consequently
- ▷ cattle
- ▷ regions
- ▷ quality
- ▷ quantity
- ▷ below
- ▷ standard
- ▷ In the end
- ▷ heavy influence

**Read the following article and compare with your writing.
As you read through, try to memorize the colored words and expressions.**

This is one of the translations for the given material. It is worth noting that many expressions used here are the professional level. Since you are assumed to write it in your own level, you should not blame yourself when you see differences between your writing and this article.

Title Environmental Change, Water Shortage
Course Environmental Science

□ Fact/Introduction

Human beings are now facing problems that were unimaginable decades ago. One of them is a shortage of water. We are experiencing the deficiency of water supply.

□ Explanation/Body

The lack of rain is in the center of this world's water shortage. The world climate has changed because of global warming. The dry season has become longer and the rainy season has become shorter. Animals and livestock relying on the rainwater for their existence are experiencing severe changes in their living environment due to this irregular and unpredictable weather pattern.

□ Assertion/Conclusion

Consequently, the body size of the cattle living in this dried land is smaller than that in other regions. Both the quality and quantity of the milk from these cattle are below standard. In the end, humans, drinking cow's milk almost everyday, are under the heavy influence of this change.

Fill in the blank by using easier and simpler vocabulary and expressions you can think of.

Try to find easier vocabulary and expressions for the blank than you have written previously. You can see what is academic and what is casual. This practice enhances your memory of the words and its practicality. You can also have a clear understanding for the synonyms.

Title Environmental Change, Water Shortage
Course Environmental Science

□ Fact/Introduction

__________ are now _____ problems that were __________ ______ ___ . One of them is a ______ of water. We are experiencing the ________ of water supply.

□ Explanation/Body

The ___ of rain is in the _____ of this world's water shortage. The world _____ has changed because of __________ . The dry season has become longer and the rainy season has become shorter. Animals and livestock _____ on the rainwater for their _______ are experiencing the _____ changes in their living ________ _____ this _______ and _________ weather pattern.

□ Assertion/Conclusion

_________ , the body size of the cattle living in this dried land is smaller than that in other _____ . Both the _____ and ______ of the milk from these cattle are below ______ . In the end, humans, drinking cow's milk almost everyday, are under the ____ influence of this change.

Guide Article

Compare the vocabulary and phrases here with those you have used previously. Many students studying English say that they do not have much vocabulary. No! That is not true at all. The reason they feel this way is that they do not have enough experiences of substituting vocabulary and phrases for others. Vocabulary and phrases takes huge parts for your writing.

Title Environmental Change, Water Shortage
Course Environmental Science

□ Fact/Introduction

Humans are now experiencing problems that were unthinkable years ago. One of them is a lack of water. We are experiencing the shortage of water supply.

□ Explanation/Body

The shortage of rain is in the middle of this world's water shortage. The world weather has changed because of greenhouse effect. The dry season has become longer and the rainy season has become shorter. Animals and livestock depending on the rainwater for their survival are experiencing the bad / serious changes in their living condition because of this unsteady and uncertain / unexpected weather pattern.

□ Assertion/Conclusion

As a result, the body size of the cattle living in this dried land is smaller than that in other places. Both the excellence / grade and the amount of the milk from these cattle are below average. In the end, humans, drinking cow's milk almost everyday, are under the massive influence of this change.

Absorb Vocabulary and Expressions

What can be used as a substitute of the word and phrase below?
Feel free to refer to the previous article.

Example Humans → **Human beings**

experiencing →

unthinkable →

lack →

shortage →

middle →

world weather →

greenhouse effect →

depending on →

survival →

bad / serious →

living condition →

because of →

unsteady →

uncertain / unexpected weather →

As a result →

places →

excellence / grade →

amount →

average →

massive influence →

Create Your Own Sentence

-Make a sentence that contains the given word and phrase.
-Use the given words for any parts of speech such as a subject, verb, object, preposition object etc.
-You can change the form of the words.

1 unimaginable

▶

2 shortage

▶

3 global warming

▶

4 dry season

▶

5 existence

▶

6. severe changes

▶

7 environment

▶

8 irregular

▶

9 unpredictable

▶

10 below standard

▶

Rephrase the colored words and phrases

Change the colored words and expressions to more difficult and academic ones!
Knowing only one word for the writing will limit your skill, so you should have the alternatives.
This practice will lead you to the state-of-art academic and formal writing.

→

> Excellent

Language skills not only put us in contact with the past,

>> Impressive & Exceptional

▶

> Excellent

they also open the people's fancy.

>> Impressive & Exceptional

▶

You can find more reading materials in this website and expand your knowledge for the rapidly changing world.

http://www.wfp.org

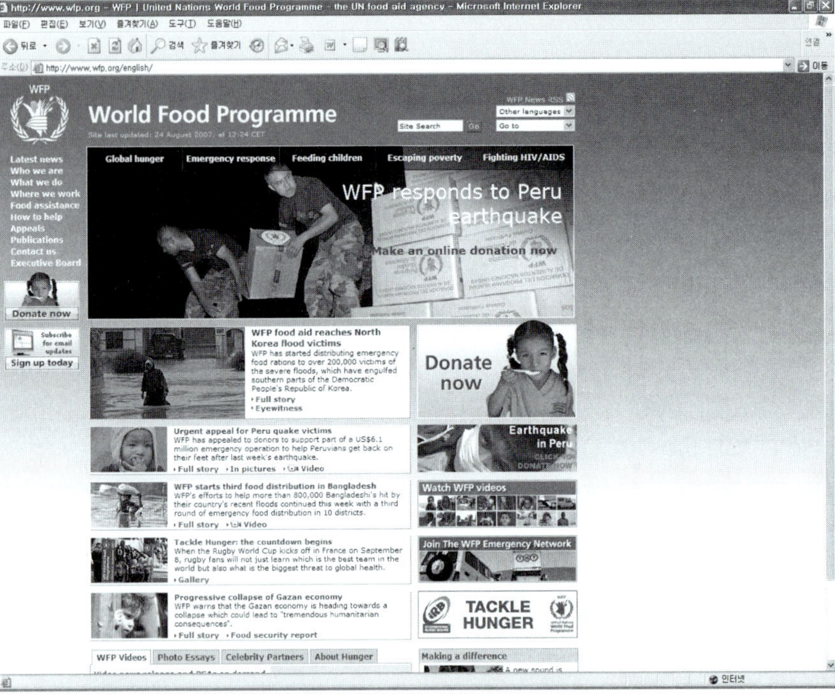

Level

Sophomore in University
TOEFL 6.0
1~1 and a half years of studying in English speaking countries

Approximate word counts

138 words

Required Skill

Some regional words and useful phrases
"ancient cave paintings," "stone knife,"
"excavated," "the upper Nile," "hilt," "illustrate,"
"the figure of," "the witnesses of."

Target 06

Higher educational institutions and elite organizations require this level of writing!

The purpose of this practice is to have you experience the high level of writing and ready for the studying in a higher educational institution. You may find it extremely difficult in choosing right words and appropriate grammar while translating the given contents.
Consult "Vocabulary You Should Know!"

Title 인간의 오래된 친구, 개
Course 인류발달사

□ Fact/Introduction

인간과 개의 관계는 그 역사가 깁니다. 인간이 지구상에 발자국을 남긴 이후로 개는 인간과 함께 있었습니다.

□ Explanation/Body

고대 동굴 벽화는 개가 인간의 사냥 동료였다는 것을 여실히 보여줍니다. 예를 들어서 Ireland의 연안에서 발견된 동굴 벽화는 다양한 개의 이미지를 담고 있습니다. 또 다른 예(例)로 나일강 상류에서 발굴된 돌칼은 손잡이 위에 개의 형상(形象)을 가지고 있습니다. 사람들이 문자를 사용하기 시작했을 때 일상생활용품에 그들의 애완동물의 이름을 포함한 여러 가지의 이름들을 새겨 넣었습니다.

□ Assertion/Conclusion

요약하면, 인류 역사 전체에 걸쳐서 우리와 함께 살고 있는 개는 인간이 어떻게 살아 남았는지에 대한 증인입니다. 비록 개에 대한 생각과 취급은 동서양에서 다를 수 있지만 그들이 친밀한 존재라는 것은 부인할 수 없는 사실입니다.

Vocabulary You Should Know!

The listed vocabulary follows the sequence of the content, not randomly mixed. This will help you find the appropriate vocabulary for your writing. Vocabulary here is not only helpful for the given writing but also leading you to the place where you are to be intelligent and educated. Remember that they are the suggestions. You can have your own choices of vocabulary for the writing which might be more acceptable than the suggested one.

- ▷ relationship
- ▷ footprints
- ▷ along with
- ▷ ancient
- ▷ cave
- ▷ vividly
- ▷ illustrate
- ▷ partners
- ▷ instance
- ▷ coast
- ▷ image
- ▷ various
- ▷ excavated
- ▷ upper Nile
- ▷ figure
- ▷ hilt
- ▷ letters
- ▷ carved
- ▷ daily goods
- ▷ pets
- ▷ throughout
- ▷ witnesses
- ▷ Even though
- ▷ treatments
- ▷ undeniable
- ▷ intimate being

**Read the following article and compare with your writing.
As you read through, try to memorize the colored words and expressions.**

This is one of the translations for the given material. It is worth noting that many expressions used here are the professional level. Since you are assumed to write it in your own level, you should not blame yourself when you see differences between your writing and this article.

Title Dogs, a Friend of Long Standing
Course History of Human Progress

□ Fact/Introduction

The history of the relationship between human beings and dogs are long. Ever since humans left their footprints on the earth, dogs were along with them.

□ Explanation/Body

Pictures from ancient cave paintings vividly illustrate that dogs were humans' hunting partners. For instance, cave paintings discovered on the coast of Ireland has an image of various dogs. A stone knife excavated in the upper Nile also has the figure of a dog on the hilt, for another example. When people began using letters, they carved various names on daily goods, including their pets' name.

□ Assertion/Conclusion

To sum up, dogs having stayed with us throughout the human history are the witnesses of how humans have survived. Even though the ideas and treatments of dogs can be different in the East and the West, it is an undeniable fact that they are intimate being

Fill in the blank by using easier and simpler vocabulary and expressions you can think of.

Try to find easier vocabulary and expressions for the blank than you have written previously. You can see what is academic and what is casual. This practice enhances your memory of the words and its practicality. You can also have a clear understanding for the synonyms.

Title Dogs, a Friend of Long Standing
Course History of Human Progress

□ Fact/Introduction

The history of the __________ between ____________ and dogs are long. _________ humans left their ________ on the ____, dogs ______________ them.

□ Explanation/Body

Pictures from ancient cave paintings ______ ________ that dogs were humans' hunting _______. For _______, cave paintings __________ on the coast of Ireland has a _____ of ______ dogs. A stone knife ________ in the upper Nile also has the ______ of a dog on the ___, for another example. When people _____ using letters, they _____ ______ names on ____ ____, including their pets' name.

□ Assertion/Conclusion

_________, dogs having ______ with us _________ the human history are the _________ of how humans have ________. ____________ the _____ and __________ of dogs can be different in the East and the West, it is a _________ fact that they are ____________.

Guide Article

Compare the vocabulary and phrases here with those you have used previously. Many students studying English say that they do not have much vocabulary. No! That is not true at all. The reason they feel this way is that they do not have enough experiences of substituting vocabulary and phrases for others. Vocabulary and phrases takes huge parts for your writing.

Title Dogs, a Friend of Long Standing
Course History of Human Progress

□ Fact/Introduction

The history of the connection between humans and dogs are long. Since humans left their traces on the ground, dogs were with them.

□ Explanation/Body

Pictures from ancient cave paintings clearly show that dogs were humans' hunting friends. For example, cave paintings found on the coast of Ireland has a picture of different dogs. A stone knife dug in the upper Nile also has the shape of a dog on the handle, for another example. When people started using letters, they put many names on everyday item, including their pets'name.

□ Assertion/Conclusion

In a word, dogs having lived with us through the human history are the observer of how humans have remained alive. Although the thoughts and cares of dogs can be different in the East and the West, it is a common fact that they are close friends.

Absorb Vocabulary and Expressions

What can be used as a substitute of the word and phrase below?
Feel free to refer to the previous article.

Example connection → **relationship**

humans →

traces →

ground →

clearly →

show →

friends →

example →

picture →

different dogs →

dug →

shape →

handle →

put many names →

everyday item →

In a word →

having lived with →

remained alive →

thoughts →

cares →

common →

close friends →

Create Your Own Sentence

-Make a sentence that contains the given word and phrase.
-Use the given words for any parts of speech such as a subject, verb, object, preposition object etc.
-You can change the form of the words.

1 relationship

▶

2 ever since

▶

3 illustrate

▶

4 excavate

▶

5 figure

▶

6. carve

▶

7 daily goods

▶

8 witnesses

▶

9 undeniable

▶

10 intimate

▶

Rephrase the colored words and phrases

Change the colored words and expressions to more difficult and academic ones!
Knowing only one word for the writing will limit your skill, so you should have the alternatives.
This practice will lead you to the state-of-art academic and formal writing.

→

> Excellent

Similarly, the cows that India's Hindus respect as holy animals

>> Impressive & Exceptional

▸

> Excellent

are regularly eaten as "hamburger meat" by hungry people in many countries.

>> Impressive & Exceptional

▸

You can find more reading materials in this website and expand your knowledge for the rapidly changing world.

http://www.mytopdogs.com/

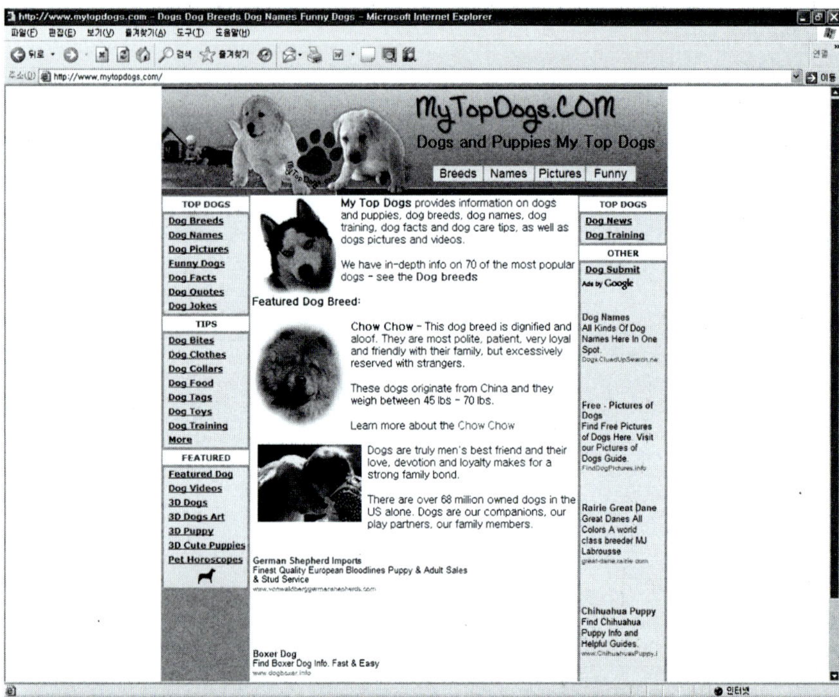

Level

Junior in University
TOEFL 6.0
2~3 years of studying in English speaking countries

Approximate word counts

141 words

Required Skill

Understanding the idiom and commonly used academic term such as "scholastic purpose," " bread of the soul," "perfection of self," "ripe experiences," "mental vision," "relaxed acceptance," "raising fears."

Target 07

Higher educational institutions and elite organizations require this level of writing!

The purpose of this practice is to have you experience the high level of writing and ready for the studying in a higher educational institution. You may find it extremely difficult in choosing right words and appropriate grammar while translating the given contents.
Consult "Vocabulary You Should Know!"

Title 여행을 통한 문화의 교류
Course 문화사회학

□ Fact/Introduction

사람들이 여행을 하는 이유는 다양합니다. 어떤 사람들은 넓은 경험을 위해서 여행을 하고 어떤 사람들은 학문적인 목적을 위해서 여행을 합니다. 많은 사람들이 여행은 영혼의 양식이고 자아(自我) 완성의 과정이라고 생각합니다.

□ Explanation/Body

빠른 대중교통을 적당한 가격으로 이용할 수 있고 교통수단의 선택도 자동차에서부터 제트기까지 확장됨에 따라 여행의 형태도 다양해졌습니다. 다양한 지역으로의 여행을 통해서 축적된 지식과 풍부한 경험으로 다른 지역에 대한 사람들의 이해도 깊어졌습니다. 그리고 이렇게 깊어진 다른 지역에 대한 이해는 외국의 물건들, 음악, 그리고 문화에 대한 우리의 시야를 바꾸어놓았습니다.

□ Assertion/Conclusion

외국의 물건에 대한 관대한 수용(受容)이 각 나라의 고유성을 침식(侵蝕)시킨다는 우려가 커지고 있기는 하지만, 그것은 우리가 지구촌에 살고 있는 한 직면(直面)해야하는 현실입니다.

Vocabulary You Should Know!

The listed vocabulary follows the sequence of the content, not randomly mixed. This will help you find the appropriate vocabulary for your writing. Vocabulary here is not only helpful for the given writing but also leading you to the place where you are to be intelligent and educated. Remember that they are the suggestions. You can have your own choices of vocabulary for the writing which might be more acceptable than the suggested one.

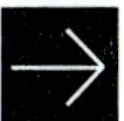

▷ reasons
▷ travel
▷ various
▷ wide
▷ scholastic
▷ purpose
▷ bread
▷ soul
▷ procedures
▷ perfection
▷ fashions
▷ varied
▷ fast public transportation
▷ available
▷ moderate
▷ mode
▷ aircraft
▷ ripe
▷ accumulated
▷ regions
▷ deepened
▷ mental vision
▷ objects
▷ relaxed
▷ acceptance
▷ materials
▷ fears
▷ erosion
▷ uniqueness
▷ present state
▷ face with
▷ global village

Read the following article and compare with your writing. As you read through, try to memorize the colored words and expressions.

This is one of the translations for the given material. It is worth noting that many expressions used here are the professional level. Since you are assumed to write it in your own level, you should not blame yourself when you see differences between your writing and this article.

Title Exchange of Culture through Traveling
Course Cultural Sociology

□ Fact/Introduction

The reasons that people travel are various. Some travel for their wide experiences and some for the scholastic purpose. Many people think that travels are the bread of the soul and the procedures of the perfection of self.

□ Explanation/Body

The fashions of traveling have become varied as the fast public transportation is available at a moderate fare and the selection of the transportation mode is extended from the cars to the jet aircraft. With the knowledge and ripe experiences accumulated through traveling over various areas, people's understanding of the different regions has deepened. And this deepened understanding about/of other areas has changed our mental vision toward foreign objects, music, and cultures.

□ Assertion/Conclusion

The relaxed acceptance of foreign materials is raising fears of the erosion of each nation's uniqueness, however, it is the present state that we should face with as long as living in a global village.

Fill in the blank by using easier and simpler vocabulary and expressions you can think of.

Try to find easier vocabulary and expressions for the blank than you have written previously. You can see what is academic and what is casual. This practice enhances your memory of the words and its practicality. You can also have a clear understanding for the synonyms.

Title Exchange of Culture through Traveling
Course Cultural Sociology

□ Fact/Introduction

The reasons that people travel are ______. Some travel for their ____ experiences and some for the ______________. Many people think that travels are the ____________ and the ________ of the _______ of self.

□ Explanation/Body

The _______ of traveling have become ______ as the fast public __________ are available at a _______ fare and the _______ of the transportation ____ is extended from the cars to the jet _____. With the ________ and ___ experiences ________ through traveling over various areas, people's understanding of the different _____ has ______. And this _______ understanding about / of other areas has changed our __________ _____ foreign _____, music, and _____.

□ Assertion/Conclusion

The _____ acceptance of foreign materials is _____ fears of the _____ of each nation's uniqueness, however, it is the present ___ that we should ___ with as long as living in a global village.

Guide Article

Compare the vocabulary and phrases here with those you have used previously. Many students studying English say that they do not have much vocabulary. No! That is not true at all. The reason they feel this way is that they do not have enough experiences of substituting vocabulary and phrases for others. Vocabulary and phrases takes huge parts for your writing.

Title Exchange of Culture through Traveling
Course Cultural Sociology

□ Fact/Introduction

The reasons that people travel are different. Some travel for their broad experiences and some for the study. Many people think that travels are the soul's bread and the steps of the completion of self.

□ Explanation/Body

The methods of traveling have become changed as the fast public vehicles/cars are available at a reasonable fare and the choice of the transportation form is extended from the cars to the jet plane. With the learning/awareness and mature experiences gathered through traveling over various areas, people's understanding of the different places has increased. And this increased understanding about/of other areas has changed our view toward foreign things, music, and culture.

□ Assertion/Conclusion

The open/generous acceptance of foreign materials is causing fears of the destruction of each nation's uniqueness, however, it is the present condition that we should meet/encounter with as long as living in a global village.

Absorb Vocabulary and Expressions

What can be used as a substitute of the word and phrase below?
Feel free to refer to the previous article.

Example different → **various**

different →

broad experiences →

study →

soul's bread →

steps →

completion →

methods →

changed →

public vehicles / cars →

reasonable fare →

choice →

transportation way →

jet plane →

learning / awareness →

mature →

gathered →

places →

increased →

our view →

foreign things →

open / generous acceptance →

causing →

destruction →

present condition →

meet / encounter with →

Create Your Own Sentence

-Make a sentence that contains the given word and phrase.
-Use the given words for any parts of speech such as a subject, verb, object, preposition object etc.
-You can change the form of the words.

1 wide experiences

▶

2 scholastic purpose

▶

3 perfection

▶

4 fashions

▶

5 fast public transportation

▶

6. moderate

▶

7 accumulate

▶

8 mental vision

▶

9 relaxed acceptance

▶

10 erosion

▶

Rephrase the colored words and phrases

Change the colored words and expressions to more difficult and academic ones!
Knowing only one word for the writing will limit your skill, so you should have the alternatives.
This practice will lead you to the state-of-art academic and formal writing.

→

\> Excellent

Studying fossil records, scientists assume that, about 2 million years ago, our remote human ancestors caught

\>> Impressive & Exceptional

▶

\> Excellent

cultural bases like the use of fire, and making tools, arms, and simple house.

\>> Impressive & Exceptional

▶

You can find more reading materials in this website and expand your knowledge for the rapidly changing world.

http://www.expedia.com

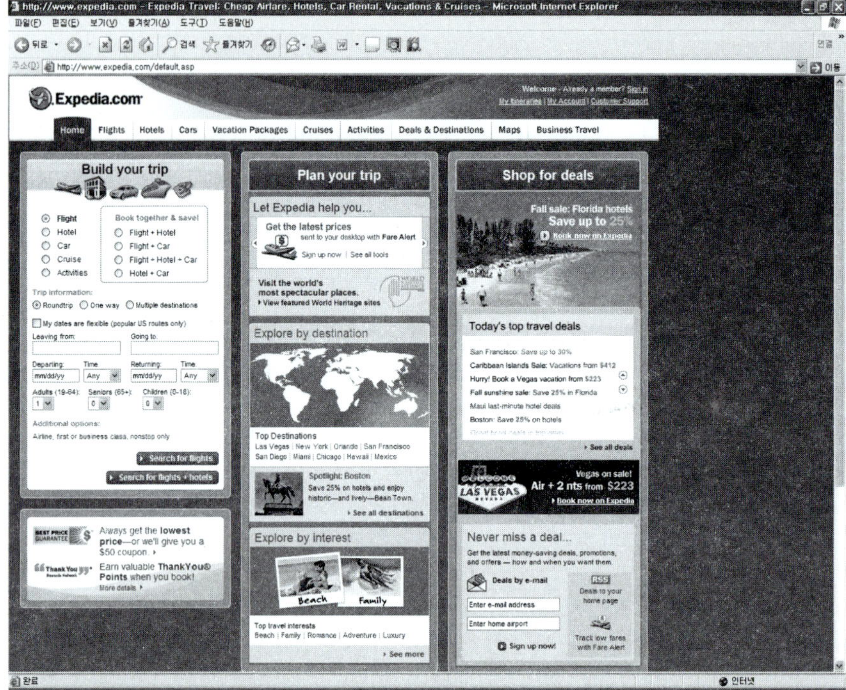

Level

Junior in University
TOEFL 6.0
2 years of studying in English speaking countries

Approximate word counts

143 words

Required Skill

Required words for the academic writing
"individualism," "ideology," "opposite," "widespread,"
"demerits," "devaluing," "underestimation,"
"hard feeling," "arisen."

Target 08

Higher educational institutions and elite organizations require this level of writing!

The purpose of this practice is to have you experience the high level of writing and ready for the studying in a higher educational institution. You may find it extremely difficult in choosing right words and appropriate grammar while translating the given contents.
Consult "Vocabulary You Should Know!"

Title 개인주의의 장단점
Course 사회학

□ Fact/Introduction

개인주의를 지지하는 사람들은 이 이념이 사생활을 보호하고 인본주의(人本主義)적인 삶으로 우리를 이끌어준다고 믿습니다. 그러나 그 반대의 견해도 쉽사리 무시할 수 없습니다.

□ Explanation/Body

개인주의의 결과에 대해서 의구심을 가지고 있는 사람들은 개인주의의 만연(漫然)이 우리의 삶에 남길 수 있는 피해를 경고하고 있습니다. 개인주의는 장점도 있고 단점도 있습니다; 개인주의의 장점은 개인의 안전을 보장하고 각(各) 개인의 노력을 인정한다는 것입니다; 개인주의의 단점은 공통체 정신의 가치를 절하(切下)하고 협동의 중요성을 과소평가한다는데 있습니다.

□ Assertion/Conclusion

이 시대에 개인주의가 번성하고 있는 이유는 사회가 예측하기 힘들어지고 공격적이 되었기 때문입니다. 사람들은 그들 자신을 위해서 안전한 장소를 가지기를 원하고 이러한 욕구가 개인주의의 성장을 부채질하게 되었습니다. 개인주의는 시대의 요구에 부합(符合)하기 위해서 발생했다고 결론을 지어도 별 무리가 없을 것입니다.

Vocabulary You Should Know!

The listed vocabulary follows the sequence of the content, not randomly mixed. This will help you find the appropriate vocabulary for your writing. Vocabulary here is not only helpful for the given writing but also leading you to the place where you are to be intelligent and educated. Remember that they are the suggestions. You can have your own choices of vocabulary for the writing which might be more acceptable than the suggested one.

- ▷ supporters
- ▷ individualism
- ▷ ideology
- ▷ humanistic
- ▷ opposite
- ▷ ignore
- ▷ question about
- ▷ outcome
- ▷ warning
- ▷ widespread
- ▷ merits
- ▷ demerits
- ▷ insurance
- ▷ safety
- ▷ recognition
- ▷ effort
- ▷ devaluing
- ▷ spirit
- ▷ cooperation
- ▷ prosperous
- ▷ era
- ▷ unpredictable
- ▷ aggressive
- ▷ secure place
- ▷ desire
- ▷ fans
- ▷ hard feeling
- ▷ needs of the times

Read the following article and compare with your writing. As you read through, try to memorize the colored words and expressions.

This is one of the translations for the given material. It is worth noting that many expressions used here are the professional level. Since you are assumed to write it in your own level, you should not blame yourself when you see differences between your writing and this article.

Title Merits and Demerits of Individualism
Course Sociology

□ Fact/Introduction

The supporters of individualism believe that this ideology protects the privacy and leads us to the humanistic life. However, the opposite view is not easy to ignore.

□ Explanation/Body

People who question about the outcome of the individualism are warning the damage that the widespread of individualism would leave on our life. Individualism has merits and demerits; merits of individualism are the insurance of the personal safety and recognition of the individual's effort; demerits of the individualism are the devaluing of the community spirit and underestimating of the importance of cooperation.

□ Assertion/Conclusion

The reason why individualism is prosperous in this era is that society has become unpredictable and aggressive. People want to have a secure place for themselves and this desire fans the growth of individualism. There would not be a hard feeling in concluding that this ideology has arisen to meet the needs of the times.

Fill in the blank by using easier and simpler vocabulary and expressions you can think of.

Try to find easier vocabulary and expressions for the blank than you have written previously. You can see what is academic and what is casual. This practice enhances your memory of the words and its practicality. You can also have a clear understanding for the synonyms.

Title Merits and Demerits of Individualism
Course Sociology

□ Fact/Introduction

The ________ of individualism believe that this ________ protects the ________ and ____ us to the ________ life. ________, the ________ ____ is not easy to ignore.

□ Explanation/Body

People who ________ about the ________ of the individualism are ________ the damage that the ________ of individualism would ____ to our life. Individualism has ________ and ________; ________ of individualism are the ________ of the personal safety and ________ of the individual's ____; ________ of the individualism are the ________ of the community ____ and ________ of the importance of ________.

□ Assertion/Conclusion

The reason why individualism is ________ in this ____ is that society ________ and ________. People want to have a ____ place for themselves and this ________ ____ the growth of individualism. There would not be a ________ in ________ that this ________ has ________ to ____ the needs of the times.

Guide Article

Compare the vocabulary and phrases here with those you have used previously. Many students studying English say that they do not have much vocabulary. No! That is not true at all. The reason they feel this way is that they do not have enough experiences of substituting vocabulary and phrases for others. Vocabulary and phrases takes huge parts for your writing.

Title Merits and Demerits of Individualism
Course Sociology

□ Fact/Introduction

The followers of individualism believe that this idea protects the private life and guides us to the humane life. But , the other thought is not easy to ignore.

□ Explanation/Body

People who doubt the result of the individualism are advising the damage that the popularity of individualism would give to our life. Individualism has good parts / advantages and bad parts / disadvantages ; good parts / advantages of individualism are the guarantee of the personal safety and acknowledgement of the individual's work ; bad parts / disadvantages of the individualism are the disrespect of the community life and undervaluing of the importance of teamwork .

□ Assertion/Conclusion

The reason why individualism is popular in this time is that society became unstable and tough . People want to have a safe place for themselves and this hope stimulates the growth of individualism. There would not be a disagreement in saying that this idea has appeared to satisfy the needs of the times.

Absorb Vocabulary and Expressions

What can be used as a substitute of the word and phrase below?
Feel free to refer to the previous article.

Example followers → **supporters**

this idea →

private life →

guides →

other thought →

doubt →

result →

advising →

popularity →

give →

good parts →

bad parts →

guarantee →

acknowledgement →

individual's work →

disrespect →

community life →

undervaluing →

teamwork →

popular →

unstable →

tough →

safe →

hope →

stimulates →

disagreement →

saying →

appeared →

satisfy →

Create Your Own Sentence

-Make a sentence that contains the given word and phrase.
-Use the given words for any parts of speech such as a subject, verb, object, preposition object etc.
-You can change the form of the words.

1 individualism

▸

2 ideology

▸

3 humanistic life

▸

4 widespread

▸

5 merits and demerits

▸

6. recognition

▸

7 underestimate

▸

8 prosperous

▸

9 unpredictable

▸

10 fans

▸

Rephrase the colored words and phrases

Change the colored words and expressions to more difficult and academic ones!
Knowing only one word for the writing will limit your skill, so you should have the alternatives.
This practice will lead you to the state-of-art academic and formal writing.

> Excellent

In a culture that has the technical skill to let one woman to give birth to a child

>> Impressive & Exceptional

▸

> Excellent

by using another woman's egg, which has been fertilized in a hospital with

>> Impressive & Exceptional

▸

> Excellent

the sperm of a absolute unknown person, how are we use the traditional

>> Impressive & Exceptional

▸

> Excellent

words being a mother and being a father?

>> Impressive & Exceptional

▸

You can find more reading materials in this website and expand your knowledge for the rapidly changing world.

http://en.wikipedia.org/wiki/Individualism

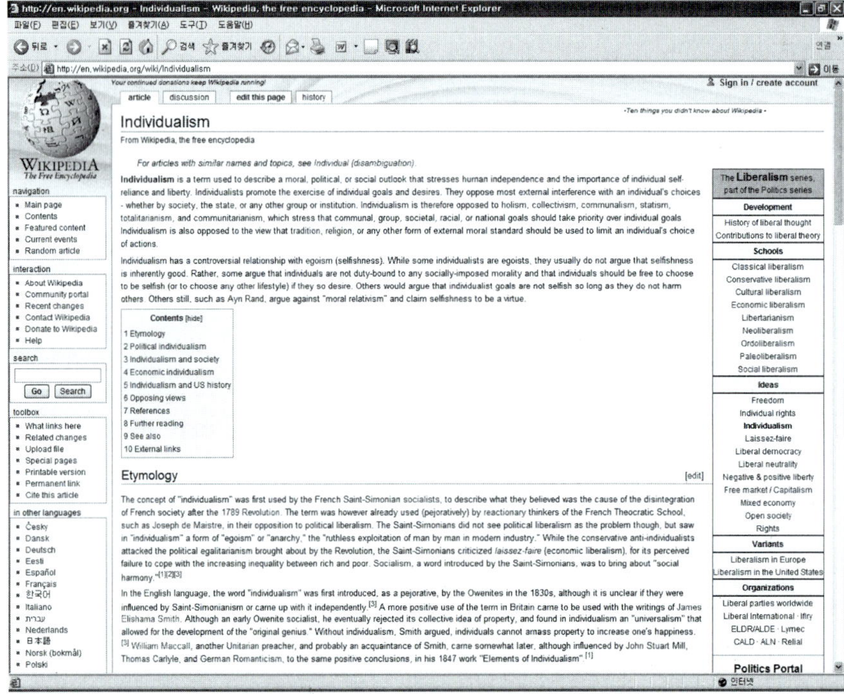

Your continued donations keep Wikipedia running!

article | discussion | edit this page | history

Sign in / create account

·Ten things you didn't know about Wikipedia·

Individualism

From Wikipedia, the free encyclopedia

For articles with similar names and topics, see Individual (disambiguation).

Individualism is a term used to describe a moral, political, or social outlook that stresses human independence and the importance of individual self-reliance and liberty. Individualists promote the exercise of individual goals and desires. They oppose most external interference with an individual's choices - whether by society, the state, or any other group or institution. Individualism is therefore opposed to holism, collectivism, communalism, statism, totalitarianism, and communitarianism, which stress that communal, group, societal, racial, or national goals should take priority over individual goals Individualism is also opposed to the view that tradition, religion, or any other form of external moral standard should be used to limit an individual's choice of actions.

Individualism has a controversial relationship with egoism (selfishness). While some individualists are egoists, they usually do not argue that selfishness is inherently good. Rather, some argue that individuals are not duty-bound to any socially-imposed morality and that individuals should be free to choose to be selfish (or to choose any other lifestyle) if they so desire. Others would argue that individualist goals are not selfish so long as they do not harm others. Others still, such as Ayn Rand, argue against "moral relativism" and claim selfishness to be a virtue.

Contents [hide]

Etymology [edit]

The concept of "individualism" was first used by the French Saint-Simonian socialists, to describe what they believed was the cause of the disintegration of French society after the 1789 Revolution. The term was however already used (pejoratively) by reactionary thinkers of the French Theocratic School, such as Joseph de Maistre, in their opposition to political liberalism. The Saint-Simonians did not see political liberalism as the problem though, but saw in "individualism" a form of "egoism" or "anarchy," the "ruthless exploitation of man by man in modern industry." While the conservative anti-individualists attacked the political egalitarianism brought about by the Revolution, the Saint-Simonians criticized *laissez-faire* (economic liberalism), for its perceived failure to cope with the increasing inequality between rich and poor. Socialism, a word introduced by the Saint-Simonians, was to bring about "social harmony."[1][2][3]

In the English language, the word "individualism" was first introduced, as a pejorative, by the Owenites in the 1830s, although it is unclear if they were influenced by Saint-Simonianism or came up with it independently.[3] A more positive use of the term in Britain came to be used with the writings of James Elishama Smith. Although an early Owenite socialist, he eventually rejected its collective idea of property, and found in individualism an "universalism" that allowed for the development of the "original genius." Without individualism, Smith argued, individuals cannot amass property to increase one's happiness.[3] William Maccall, another Unitarian preacher, and probably an acquaintance of Smith, came somewhat later, although influenced by John Stuart Mill, Thomas Carlyle, and German Romanticism, to the same positive conclusions, in his 1847 work "Elements of Individualism".[1]

The **Liberalism** series, part of the Politics series

Development
History of liberal thought
Contributions to liberal theory

Schools
Classical liberalism
Conservative liberalism
Cultural liberalism
Economic liberalism
Libertarianism
Neoliberalism
Ordoliberalism
Paleoliberalism
Social liberalism

Ideas
Freedom
Individual rights
Individualism
Laissez-faire
Liberal democracy
Liberal neutrality
Negative & positive liberty
Free market / Capitalism
Mixed economy
Open society
Rights

Variants
Liberalism in Europe
Liberalism in the United States

Organizations
Liberal parties worldwide
Liberal International · lfiry
ELDR/ALDE · Lymec
CALD · ALN · Relial

Politics Portal

WIKIPEDIA
The Free Encyclopedia

navigation
- Main page
- Contents
- Featured content
- Current events
- Random article

interaction
- About Wikipedia
- Community portal
- Recent changes
- Contact Wikipedia
- Donate to Wikipedia
- Help

search

Go | Search

toolbox
- What links here
- Related changes
- Upload file
- Special pages
- Printable version
- Permanent link
- Cite this article

in other languages
- Česky
- Dansk
- Deutsch
- Eesti
- Español
- Français
- 한국어
- Italiano
- עברית
- Nederlands
- 日本語
- Norsk (bokmål)
- Polski

Level

Sophomore in University
TOEFL 6.0
1~2 years of studying in English speaking countries

Approximate word counts

133 words

Required Skill

General knowledge of some Academic words such as, "permanent settlement," "survival rate," "farming technique," "suitable," "long-term," "raising," "turning point," "decades," "huge influence," "to sum up," "accelerate," "expansion."

Target 09

Higher educational institutions and elite organizations require this level of writing!

The purpose of this practice is to have you experience the high level of writing and ready for the studying in a higher educational institution. You may find it extremely difficult in choosing right words and appropriate grammar while translating the given contents.
Consult "Vocabulary You Should Know!"

Title 정착생활을 가능하게 한 세가지 요소
Course 인류학

□ Fact/Introduction

영구적인 정착지에서 사는 것이 생존률을 높이고 농경(農耕)기술을 발달시킬 기회를 준다는 것을 사람들이 깨달음에 따라 그들은 장기(長期) 거주를 위한 적절한 장소를 찾기 위해 노력했습니다.

□ Explanation/Body

그들이 강 근처에 정착했을 때 그들은 농작물을 재배하고 가축을 기르는 것이 편안하다는 것을 깨달았습니다. 강 주변에 주거지(住居址)를 세우는 것은 그들에게 있어서 전환점이 되었습니다; 즉, 그들은 한 장소에서 수십 년 동안 살 수 있게 되었습니다. 이러한 삶의 형태는 거대한 영향을 가져왔습니다. 게다가, 사람들은 땅을 뒤엎기 위해서 쟁기를 발명했습니다. 농사일을 위한 쟁기의 소개는 사람들이 밭에서 더 빨리 그리고 더 쉽게 일하도록 했습니다.

□ Assertion/Conclusion

요약하면, 정착하기 위한 장소를 찾는 것, 강 근처에 사는 것의 선호(選好) 그리고 농기구의 사용 이 모두가 영구적인 정착지의 확장을 가속화했습니다.

Vocabulary You Should Know!

The listed vocabulary follows the sequence of the content, not randomly mixed. This will help you find the appropriate vocabulary for your writing. Vocabulary here is not only helpful for the given writing but also leading you to the place where you are to be intelligent and educated. Remember that they are the suggestions. You can have your own choices of vocabulary for the writing which might be more acceptable than the suggested one.

- ▷ realized
- ▷ permanent
- ▷ settlement
- ▷ enhanced
- ▷ rate
- ▷ suitable
- ▷ long-term
- ▷ convenience
- ▷ crops
- ▷ residential
- ▷ areas
- ▷ turning point
- ▷ were able to
- ▷ huge
- ▷ influences
- ▷ In addition
- ▷ invented
- ▷ plows
- ▷ turn
- ▷ introduction
- ▷ farm work
- ▷ allowed
- ▷ field
- ▷ To sum up
- ▷ favoring
- ▷ tools
- ▷ accelerated
- ▷ expansion

Read the following article and compare with your writing. As you read through, try to memorize the colored words and expressions.

This is one of the translations for the given material. It is worth noting that many expressions used here are the professional level. Since you are assumed to write it in your own level, you should not blame yourself when you see differences between your writing and this article.

Title Three Elements Making Possible for a Permanent Settlement
Course Anthropology

□ Fact/Introduction

As people realized that living in a permanent settlement enhanced the survival rate and gave a chance to develop the farming techniques, they tried to look for suitable places for their long-term settlements.

□ Explanation/Body

They saw the convenience of raising crops and cattle when they settled near the river. Building residential site around the river became a turning point for them; that is, they were able to live in a place for decades. This living pattern brought huge influences. In addition, people invented plows to turn the soil. The introduction of the plows for the farm work allowed people to work faster and easier in the field.

□ Assertion/Conclusion

To sum up, searching for places to settle down, favoring to live near the river, and using farming tools altogether accelerated the expansion of the permanent settlement.

Fill in the blank by using easier and simpler vocabulary and expressions you can think of.

Try to find easier vocabulary and expressions for the blank than you have written previously. You can see what is academic and what is casual. This practice enhances your memory of the words and its practicality. You can also have a clear understanding for the synonyms.

Title Three Elements Making Possible for a Permanent Settlement
Course Anthropology

□ Fact/Introduction

As people ________ that living in a permanent __________ __________ the survival ___ and gave a chance to develop the farming ________, they tried to look for _______ places for their long-term _________.

□ Explanation/Body

They ____ the __________ of ______ crops and _____ when they ______ near the river. ________ residential ___ around the river became an ______ point for them; that is, they __________ live in a place for ______. This living ______ brought ____ influences. In addition, people ________ plows to ____ the ___. The introduction of the plows for the farm work ______ people _______ faster and easier in the field.

□ Assertion/Conclusion

To sum up, ________ for places to settle down, ________ to live near the river, and using farming tools altogether __________ the _________ of the permanent ________.

Guide Article

Compare the vocabulary and phrases here with those you have used previously. Many students studying English say that they do not have much vocabulary. No! That is not true at all. The reason they feel this way is that they do not have enough experiences of substituting vocabulary and phrases for others. Vocabulary and phrases takes huge parts for your writing.

Title Three Elements Making Possible for a Permanent Settlement
Course Anthropology

□ Fact/Introduction

As people understood that living in a permanent place raise the survival chance and gave a chance to develop the farming skills , they tried to look for right places for their long-term house .

□ Explanation/Body

They realized the easy way of cultivating crops and cows when they lived near the river. Making residential areas around the river became an important point for them; that is, they could live in a place for 10 years . This living style brought big influences. In addition, people made plows to cultivate the land . The introduction of the plows for the farm work made people work faster and easier in the field.

□ Assertion/Conclusion

To sum up, looking for places to settle down, agreeing to live near the river, and using farming tools altogether sped up the spreading of the permanent living place .

Absorb Vocabulary and Expressions

What can be used as a substitute of the word and phrase below?
Feel free to refer to the previous article.

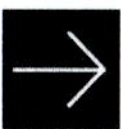
Example understood → **realized**

place →

raise →

survival chance →

right places →

long-term house →

realized →

easy way →

cultivating crops →

cows →

making →

important point →

style →

big influences →

made →

cultivate the soil →

looking →

agreeing →

sped up →

spreading →

living place →

Create Your Own Sentence

-Make a sentence that contains the given word and phrase.
-Use the given words for any parts of speech such as a subject, verb, object, preposition object etc.
-You can change the form of the words.

1 permanent settlement

▸

2 enhance

▸

3 long-term

▸

4 residential

▸

5 turning point

▸

6. invent

▸

7 farm work

▸

8 allow

▸

9 favor

▸

10 accelerate

▸

Rephrase the colored words and phrases

Change the colored words and expressions to more difficult and academic ones!
Knowing only one word for the writing will limit your skill, so you should have the alternatives.
This practice will lead you to the state-of-art academic and formal writing.

> **Excellent**

The citizen's rights, women's freedom, and movements that are against a war

>> **Impressive & Exceptional**

▶

> **Excellent**

emphasized ways in which political, economic, army, and technological

>> **Impressive & Exceptional**

▶

> **Excellent**

factor of "the system" set the outline of people's lives.

>> **Impressive & Exceptional**

▶

You can find more reading materials in this website and expand your knowledge for the rapidly changing world.

http://www.rudimentsofwisdom.com

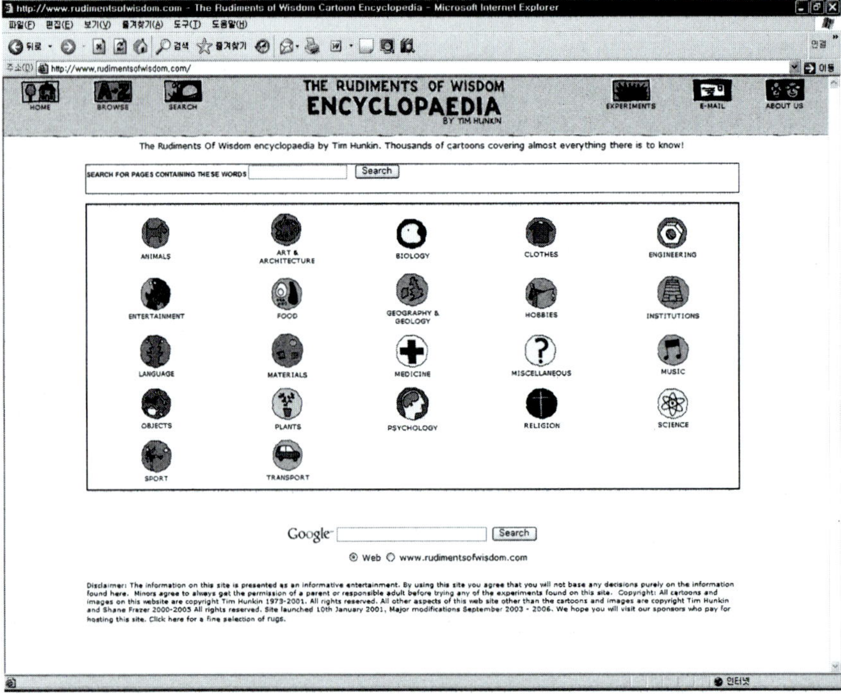

Level

Senior in University
TOEFL 6.0
3~4 years of studying in English speaking countries

Approximate word counts

144 words

Required Skill

Memorizing commonly used academic expressions such as, "struggle," "regarding," "ongoing," "dawn of mass media," "profitable means," "are exposed to," "restraint," "alternative choice," "upper hand," "induce," "appeal," "maintained."

Target 10

Higher educational institutions and elite organizations require this level of writing!

The purpose of this practice is to have you experience the high level of writing and ready for the studying in a higher educational institution. You may find it extremely difficult in choosing right words and appropriate grammar while translating the given contents.
Consult "Vocabulary You Should Know!"

Title 광고, 성적인 메시지, 부모들의 염려
Course 대중매체

□ Fact/Introduction

성(性)적 논쟁에 관한 부모들과 대중매체 사이의 싸움은 몇 십년간 진행되어 오고 있습니다. 물건을 팔기위한 성(性)의 사용이 늘어남에 따라 그들의 자녀를 교육시켜야 하는 부모들의 책임은 더 커지고 더 어려워졌습니다.

□ Explanation/Body

대중매체의 시작 이래로 광고주들은 성(性)이 장사가 된다는 것을 알아냈습니다. 그들은 이 이익이 되는 수단을 향수에서부터, 음식, 장신구 그리고 심지어 휴가상품에까지 무엇이든 팔기위해서 사용해 왔습니다. 아이들은 영화, 텔레비전, 음악 그리고 인터넷의 형태로 광고주들의 대중매체 사용을 통해서 잡다한 성(性) 정보에 노출되어 있습니다. 부모들은 그들의 아이들에게 자제하라고 몰아세우는 것만이 능사(能事)가 아니라는 것을 깨닫게 되었지만 확실한 대안(代案)이 그들에게 없는 것이 문제입니다.

□ Assertion/Conclusion

안타깝지만 현실적으로, 성(性)적인 메시지가 구매욕을 부추기는데 우위를 차지하는 한 이러한 싸움은 지속될 것이고 성(性)의 호소는 유지될 것입니다.

Vocabulary You Should Know!

The listed vocabulary follows the sequence of the content, not randomly mixed. This will help you find the appropriate vocabulary for your writing. Vocabulary here is not only helpful for the given writing but also leading you to the place where you are to be intelligent and educated. Remember that they are the suggestions. You can have your own choices of vocabulary for the writing which might be more acceptable than the suggested one.

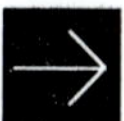

- ▷ struggle
- ▷ mass media
- ▷ regarding ~ of
- ▷ issue
- ▷ sexuality
- ▷ ongoing
- ▷ decades
- ▷ growing
- ▷ products
- ▷ responsibility
- ▷ educate
- ▷ greater
- ▷ harder
- ▷ dawn of ~
- ▷ profitable means
- ▷ accessories
- ▷ vacation packages
- ▷ be exposed to
- ▷ mixed
- ▷ signals
- ▷ the forms of ~
- ▷ come to realize
- ▷ urging
- ▷ restraint
- ▷ absence
- ▷ alternative
- ▷ sadly
- ▷ surely
- ▷ the message of ~
- ▷ upper hand
- ▷ induce
- ▷ interest
- ▷ continue
- ▷ appeal
- ▷ be maintained

Read the following article and compare with your writing. As you read through, try to memorize the colored words and expressions.

This is one of the translations for the given material. It is worth noting that many expressions used here are the professional level. Since you are assumed to write it in your own level, you should not blame yourself when you see differences between your writing and this article.

Title Advertisements, Messages of Sex, Parents' worry
Course Mass Communication

□ Fact/Introduction

The struggle between parents and mass media regarding the issue of sexuality has been ongoing for many decades. With the growing use of sex to sell products, the parent's responsibility to educate their children has become greater and harder.

□ Explanation/Body

Since the dawn of mass media advertisers have discovered that sex sells. They have used this profitable means to sell anything from perfumes, food, accessories, and even to vacation packages. Children are exposed to the mixed signals of sex through advertisers' use of mass media in the forms of movies, television, music and the Internet. Even though parents come to realize that urging restraint to their children is not the best answer, the absence of the reliable, alternative choice for them is the problem.

□ Assertion/Conclusion

Sadly but surely, as long as the message of sex has the upper hand to induce customers' interest, this struggle will continue and its appeal will be maintained.

Fill in the blank by using easier and simpler vocabulary and expressions you can think of.

Try to find easier vocabulary and expressions for the blank than you have written previously. You can see what is academic and what is casual. This practice enhances your memory of the words and its practicality. You can also have a clear understanding for the synonyms.

Title Advertisements, Messages of Sex, Parents'worry
Course Mass Communication

□ Fact/Introduction

The ________ between parents and mass ______ ________ the _____ of ________ has been ________ for many decades. With the growing use of sex to sell ________, the parent's ____________ to _______ their children has become greater and harder.

□ Explanation/Body

Since the _____ of mass media advertisers have _________ that sex sells. They have used this ________ ______ to sell anything from perfumes, food, _________, and even to vacation packages. Children are exposed to the _____ ______ of sex through advertisers' use of mass media in the forms of movies, television, music and the Internet. ___________ parents come to ______ that _______ _______ to their children is not the ____ answer, the _______ of the ______, ________ choice for them is the problem.

□ Assertion/Conclusion

_____________, as long as the message of sex has the _________ to ______ customers' interest, this _______ will ________ and its ______ will be _________.

Guide Article

Compare the vocabulary and phrases here with those you have used previously. Many students studying English say that they do not have much vocabulary. No! That is not true at all. The reason they feel this way is that they do not have enough experiences of substituting vocabulary and phrases for others. Vocabulary and phrases takes huge parts for your writing.

Title Advertisements, Messages of Sex, Parents'worry
Course Mass Communication

□ **Fact/Introduction**

The fight between parents and mass communication about the problem of sex has been continued for many decades. With the growing use of sex to sell goods , the parent's role/job/charge/duty to teach their children has become greater and harder.

□ **Explanation/Body**

Since the beginning of mass media advertisers have found that sex sells. They have used this moneymaking method to sell anything from perfumes, food, personal ornaments , and even to vacation packages. Children are exposed to the unclear signs of sex through advertisers' use of mass media in the forms of movies, television, music and the Internet. Although parents come to understand that pushing self-control to their children is not the perfect/fine/good answer, the nonexistence of the dependable , substitute/different/another choice for them is the problem.

□ **Assertion/Conclusion**

Unfortunately , as long as the message of sex has the advantage to draw customers' interest, this fight will last/go on and its attraction will be kept .

Absorb Vocabulary and Expressions

What can be used as a substitute of the word and phrase below?
Feel free to refer to the previous article.

Example fight → **struggle**

communication →

about →

problem →

sex →

continued →

goods →

role / job / charge / duty →

teach →

beginning →

found →

moneymaking method →

personal ornaments →

unclear signs →

Although →

understand →

pushing →

self-control →

perfect / fine / good →

nonexistence →

dependable →

substitute / different / another →

Unfortunately →

advantage →

draw →

fight →

last / go on →

attraction →

kept →

Create Your Own Sentence

-Make a sentence that contains the given word and phrase.
-Use the given words for any parts of speech such as a subject, verb, object, preposition object etc.
-You can change the form of the words.

1 struggle between

▸

2 regarding

▸

3 responsibility

▸

4 greater and harder

▸

5 profitable means

▸

6. be exposed to

▸

7 urge

▸

8 alternative

▸

9 upper hand

▸

10 induce

▸

Rephrase the colored words and phrases

Change the colored words and expressions to more difficult and academic ones!
Knowing only one word for the writing will limit your skill, so you should have the alternatives.
This practice will lead you to the state-of-art academic and formal writing.

> Excellent

We describe children and grown-up people in different ways,

>> Impressive & Exceptional

▶

> Excellent

with "careless" children watched over by "reliable" adults.

>> Impressive & Exceptional

▶

You can find more reading materials in this website and expand your knowledge for the rapidly changing world.

http://www.ltcconline.net/lukas/gender/sexviolence/sexualviolence.htm

SEXUAL VIOLENCE

Background: John Stoltenberg (1997b) develops an important critique of male heterosexuality by focusing on the need for males to take an active role in creating non-violent relationships. He discusses the need of consent, mutuality and respect in sexual and personal relationships. He suggests that men can work to not have their sexuality manipulated by the pornography industry, drugs or alcohol and that men "start choosing now not to fixate on fucking" (1997b:227). This last quote situates the discussion of ads that emphasize sexual violence against women in the terrain of the personal. An ultimate goal of a free gender society is to alter the media landscape and eliminate such ads from it, but a more immediate goal allows men to specifically alter their psychological and physical approaches to women, or men, in heterosexual and homosexual relationships. One of the ultimate questions that must be asked when studying gender and popular imagery is that of causality—what is the impact of images on people's lives and their relationships? Of course, it is too simplistic to assume a "Judas Priest Factor"—that exposure to a particular form of popular culture will result in a specific behavioral reaction in individuals—but there is remarkable evidence that the ads present in our society do impact our psychological understandings of gender and sexuality. As Lindsey suggests in highlighting previous research on this subject (Rudman and Verdi 1993; Lanis and Covell 1995), "males exposed to ads where females are portrayed as sex objects are more accepting of rape-supportive attitudes and predictive of subjective levels of exploitation" (1997:315). Clearly, the construction of masculinity involves a dual defamation of women as sex objects and a maintenance of male sexual superiority (cf. Hood 1995).

Focus on the Ads: Consider the disturbing S&M image in 10. This is not an image from a smut magazine, it's a mainstream fashion image! Have a look at images 16, 17, 18, 19, 20. What are the implications for a democratic society when we are telling our citizens that its alright to sexually touch and assault women (does the current Arnold Schwarzenegger controversy seem relevant here?) Images 33, 36 and 37 are very troubling, what type of society can we aspire to create when we are not valuing the right of a woman, or anyone, to SAY NO!? Then there is the issue of ad 64, which for me is one of the most disgusting images of popular culture I have seen. Can we do better?

A sentence can be translated into various ways because each person has a different grammar level and a vocabulary skill.
There should be an idea of appropriateness of the word usage and grammar application. However, it may not be wise to determine which sentence is linguistically right or wrong as long as a sentence you have created conveys the communicative message.
Do not think that this Guideline is a concrete and fixed answer!
What you have written may be better than the Guideline presented here.

Guideline

Target 01

Rephrase the colored words and phrases

We believe that people should be free to act without unreasonable interference from anyone else.

Target 02

Rephrase the colored words and phrases

Almost half of the world's people live in the fifty least-developed countries, nations with little industrialization in which severe poverty is the rule.

Target 03

Rephrase the colored words and phrases

As factory sprouted up across English and the Europe continent, cities grew to unprecedented size.

Target 04

Rephrase the colored words and phrases

Although people sometimes quip that "money won't buy happiness," most eagerly pursue wealth all the same.

Target 05

Rephrase the colored words and phrases

Language skills not only place us in touch with the past, they also unlock the human imagination.

Target 06

Rephrase the colored words and phrases

Likewise, the cows that India's Hindus revere as sacred animals are routinely consumed as "hamburger meat" by hungry people in many countries.

Target 07

Rephrase the colored words and phrases

Studying fossil records, scientists conclude that, about 2 million years ago, our distant human forefather grasped cultural fundamentals like the use of fire, and making tools, weapons, and simple shelters.

Target 08

Rephrase the colored words and phrases

In a culture that has the technical ability to allow one woman to give birth to a child by using another woman's egg, which has been fertilized in a laboratory with the sperm of a total stranger, how are we apply the traditional terms motherhood and fatherhood?

Target 09

Rephrase the colored words and phrases

The civil rights, women's liberation, and antiwar movements highlighted ways in which political, economic, military, and technological elements of "the system" set the contours of people's lives.

Target 10

Rephrase the colored words and phrases

We define children and adult in contrasting ways, with "irresponsible" children looked after by "responsible" adults.

TOP
LEVEL
WRITING
SENSE
THE TWO
For Elite Group

II

TOP
LEVEL
WRITING
SENSE
THE TWO

For Elite Group

II

TOP
LEVEL
WRITING
SENSE
THE TWO

For Elite Group

II